In the past few years, archit..... ....
around the world have found in China the perfect
location to develop their architecture, thanks to
major changes taking place throughout the country. Due to restrictions and limitations in European
and American cities, Shanghai—with its seemingly
boundless possibilities—represents a new opportunity for architecture and urbanism.

While other Chinese cities such as Beijing are
transforming their appearance with new major
buildings, Shanghai, with Expo 2010 on the horizon,
is immersed in something much deeper: a transformation of its physical structure that reconsiders
fundamental relationships within the city.

The transformation of Shanghai is unique in
its speed, scale, and politics. In image and text,
Shanghai Transforming studies the facts:
physical, economic, social and environmental—
equipping readers to untangle and understand
these complex processes, and in so doing, to
explore possibilities for the future.   Iker Gil, ed.

Shanghai Transforming

The changing physical, economic, social and environmental conditions of a global metropolis

Iker Gil, ed.

Shanghai Transforming

World's Twenty Largest Urban Agglomerations
1980-2010

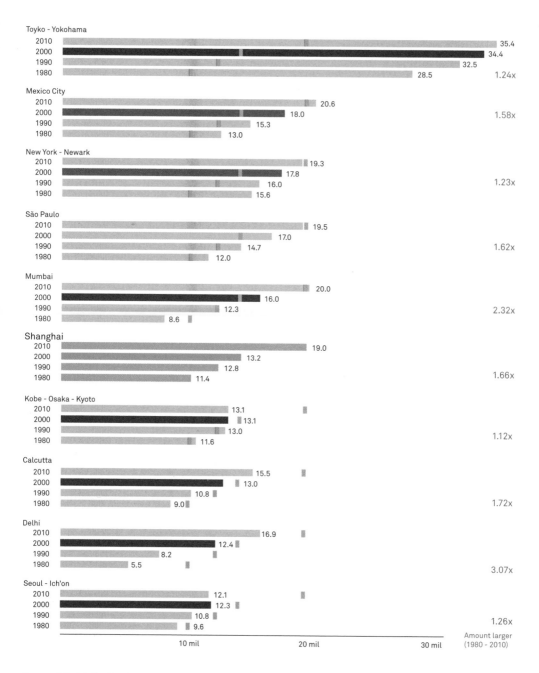

Toyko - Yokohama
- 2010 — 35.4
- 2000 — 34.4
- 1990 — 32.5
- 1980 — 28.5 — 1.24x

Mexico City
- 2010 — 20.6
- 2000 — 18.0
- 1990 — 15.3
- 1980 — 13.0 — 1.58x

New York - Newark
- 2010 — 19.3
- 2000 — 17.8
- 1990 — 16.0
- 1980 — 15.6 — 1.23x

São Paulo
- 2010 — 19.5
- 2000 — 17.0
- 1990 — 14.7
- 1980 — 12.0 — 1.62x

Mumbai
- 2010 — 20.0
- 2000 — 16.0
- 1990 — 12.3
- 1980 — 8.6 — 2.32x

Shanghai
- 2010 — 19.0
- 2000 — 13.2
- 1990 — 12.8
- 1980 — 11.4 — 1.66x

Kobe - Osaka - Kyoto
- 2010 — 13.1
- 2000 — 13.1
- 1990 — 13.0
- 1980 — 11.6 — 1.12x

Calcutta
- 2010 — 15.5
- 2000 — 13.0
- 1990 — 10.8
- 1980 — 9.0 — 1.72x

Delhi
- 2010 — 16.9
- 2000 — 12.4
- 1990 — 8.2
- 1980 — 5.5 — 3.07x

Seoul - Ich'on
- 2010 — 12.1
- 2000 — 12.3
- 1990 — 10.8
- 1980 — 9.6 — 1.26x

10 mil   20 mil   30 mil   Amount larger (1980 - 2010)

Source: United Nations World Urbanization Prospects: The 2006 Revision Population Database.
http://esa.un.org/unup (accessed Sept. 20, 2007)

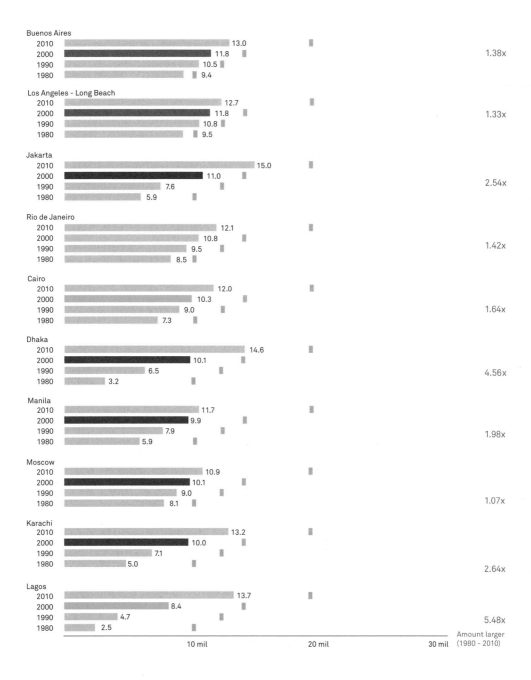

Buenos Aires
- 2010 — 13.0
- 2000 — 11.8
- 1990 — 10.5
- 1980 — 9.4

1.38x

Los Angeles - Long Beach
- 2010 — 12.7
- 2000 — 11.8
- 1990 — 10.8
- 1980 — 9.5

1.33x

Jakarta
- 2010 — 15.0
- 2000 — 11.0
- 1990 — 7.6
- 1980 — 5.9

2.54x

Rio de Janeiro
- 2010 — 12.1
- 2000 — 10.8
- 1990 — 9.5
- 1980 — 8.5

1.42x

Cairo
- 2010 — 12.0
- 2000 — 10.3
- 1990 — 9.0
- 1980 — 7.3

1.64x

Dhaka
- 2010 — 14.6
- 2000 — 10.1
- 1990 — 6.5
- 1980 — 3.2

4.56x

Manila
- 2010 — 11.7
- 2000 — 9.9
- 1990 — 7.9
- 1980 — 5.9

1.98x

Moscow
- 2010 — 10.9
- 2000 — 10.1
- 1990 — 9.0
- 1980 — 8.1

1.07x

Karachi
- 2010 — 13.2
- 2000 — 10.0
- 1990 — 7.1
- 1980 — 5.0

2.64x

Lagos
- 2010 — 13.7
- 2000 — 8.4
- 1990 — 4.7
- 1980 — 2.5

5.48x

10 mil   20 mil   30 mil   Amount larger
                                       (1980 - 2010)

China's Ten Largest Urban Agglomerations

1980–2010

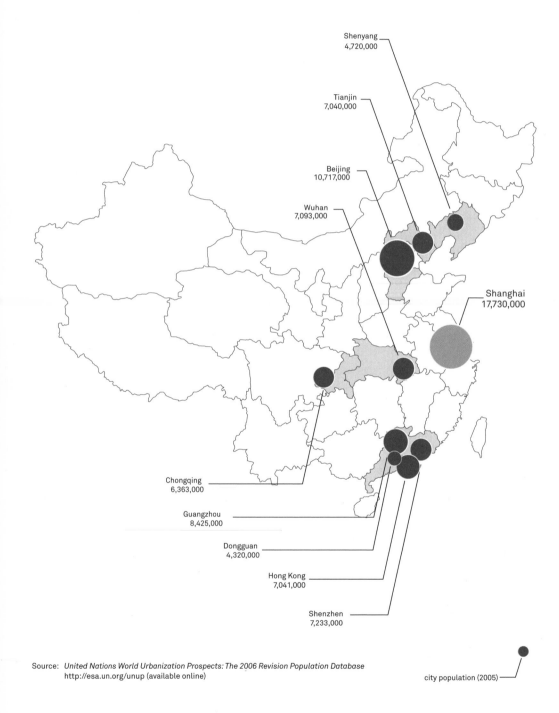

Shenyang
4,720,000

Tianjin
7,040,000

Beijing
10,717,000

Wuhan
7,093,000

Shanghai
17,730,000

Chongqing
6,363,000

Guangzhou
8,425,000

Dongguan
4,320,000

Hong Kong
7,041,000

Shenzhen
7,233,000

Source: *United Nations World Urbanization Prospects: The 2006 Revision Population Database*
          http://esa.un.org/unup (available online)

city population (2005)

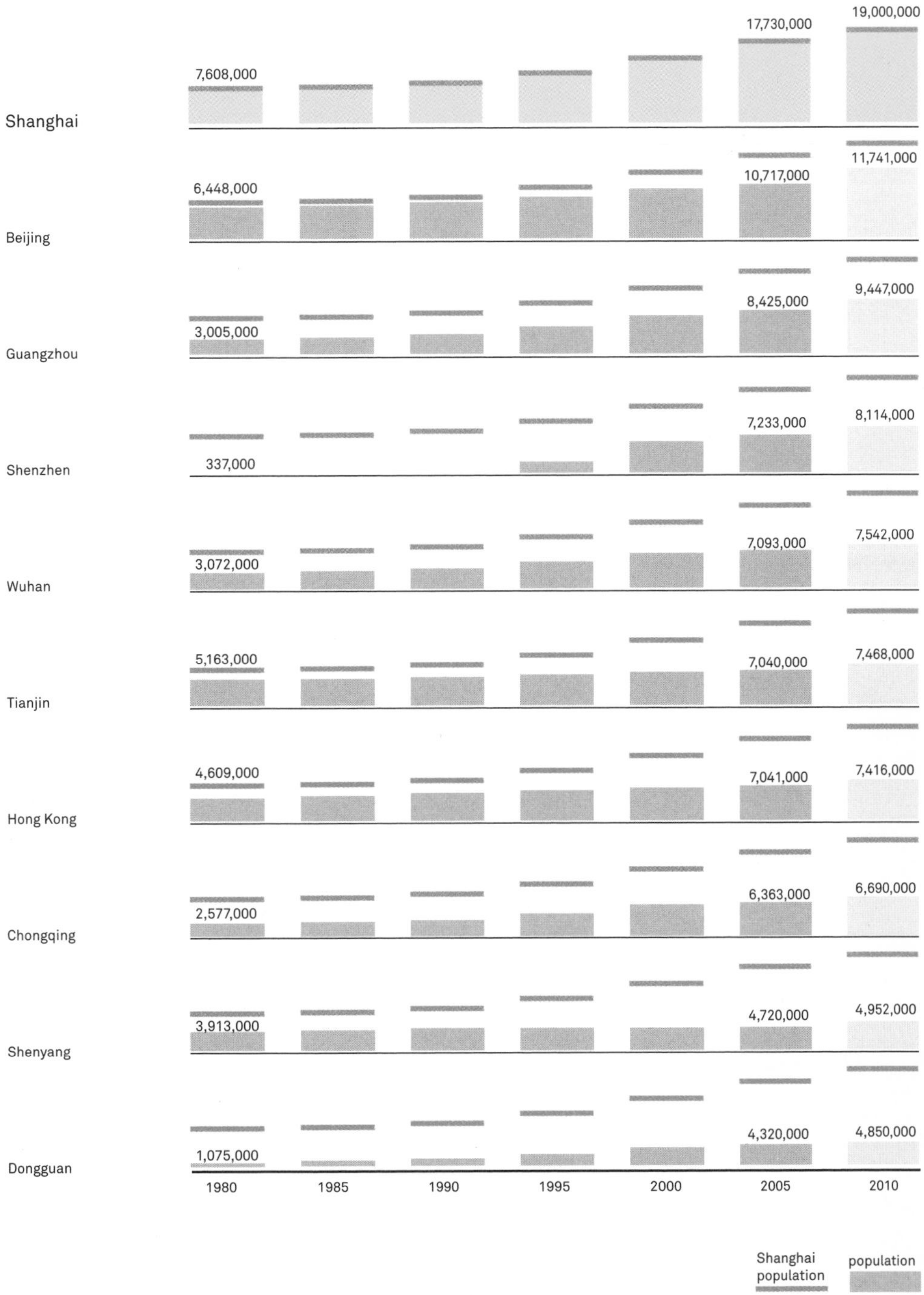

	1980	1985	1990	1995	2000	2005	2010
Shanghai	7,608,000					17,730,000	19,000,000
Beijing	6,448,000					10,717,000	11,741,000
Guangzhou	3,005,000					8,425,000	9,447,000
Shenzhen	337,000					7,233,000	8,114,000
Wuhan	3,072,000					7,093,000	7,542,000
Tianjin	5,163,000					7,040,000	7,468,000
Hong Kong	4,609,000					7,041,000	7,416,000
Chongqing	2,577,000					6,363,000	6,690,000
Shenyang	3,913,000					4,720,000	4,952,000
Dongguan	1,075,000					4,320,000	4,850,000

Shanghai population

population

17

Shanghai Region

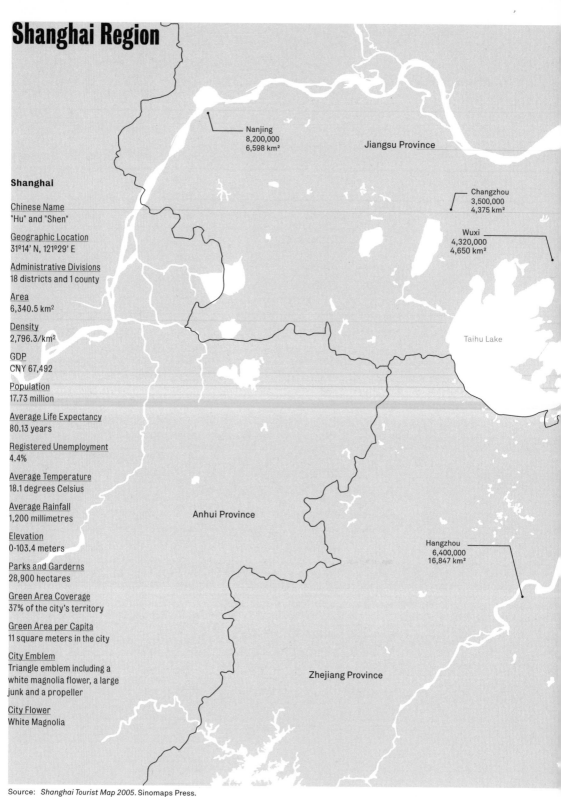

Shanghai

Chinese Name
"Hu" and "Shen"

Geographic Location
31º14' N, 121º29' E

Administrative Divisions
18 districts and 1 county

Area
6,340.5 km²

Density
2,796.3/km²

GDP
CNY 67,492

Population
17.73 million

Average Life Expectancy
80.13 years

Registered Unemployment
4.4%

Average Temperature
18.1 degrees Celsius

Average Rainfall
1,200 millimetres

Elevation
0-103.4 meters

Parks and Gardens
28,900 hectares

Green Area Coverage
37% of the city's territory

Green Area per Capita
11 square meters in the city

City Emblem
Triangle emblem including a
white magnolia flower, a large
junk and a propeller

City Flower
White Magnolia

Nanjing
8,200,000
6,598 km²

Jiangsu Province

Changzhou
3,500,000
4,375 km²

Wuxi
4,320,000
4,650 km²

Taihu Lake

Anhui Province

Hangzhou
6,400,000
16,847 km²

Zhejiang Province

Source: *Shanghai Tourist Map 2005*. Sinomaps Press.
China Statistical Yearbook 2006. National Bureau of Statistics of China.
(Beijing: China Statistics Press, 2006) Table 1.1 Also available online and as a CD-ROM.
Shanghai.gov. 2007. Shanghai Municipal Government 30 January 2008 http://www.shanghai.gov.cn
(accessed June 15 2007).

Yellow Sea

Nantong
7,7000,000
8,001 km²

Yangtze River

Suzhou
6,062,200
8,488 km²

Shanghai
17,730,000
6,340.5 km²

Hangzhou Bay

Qiangting River

Shaoxing
4,347,200
8,256 km²

Ningbo
5,527,000
9,365 km²

East China Sea

N

0 1   5   10   25 km

Physical Transformation

Inner Ring

Bund

People's Square

Huangpu River

Suzhou Creek

Xujiahui

Inner Ring Road

Humna

Lujiazui

Source: *Summary of the Comprehensive Plan of Shanghai (1999-2020).* Shanghai Urban Planning Administration Bureau. Shanghai Urban Planning and Design Research Institute.

Outer Ring

Huangpu River

Outer Ring Road

Waqaoqiao

Jiangwan - Wujiaochang

Zhenru

Jinqiao

Suzhou Creek

Hongqiao

Zhangjing

Caohejing

Humna
Lujiazui

Xujiahui

Inner Ring Road

N

0 1   5   10   20 km

Source: *Summary of the Comprehensive Plan of Shanghai (1999-2020)*. Shanghai Urban Planning
Administration Bureau. Shanghai Urban Planning and Design Research Institute.

Administrative Divisions

Chongming

Jiading

Baoshan

Yangtze River

Putuo

Zhabei

Hongkou

Yangpu

Pudong

Huangpu River

Huangpu

Luwan

Jing'an

Xuhui

Changing

Minhang

Nanhui

Fengxian

Sonjiang

Jinshan

Qingpu

Hangzhou Bay

N

0 1 5 10 20 km

Source: *Summary of the Comprehensive Plan of Shanghai (1999-2020)*. Shanghai Urban Planning
Administration Bureau. Shanghai Urban Planning and Design Research Institute.

Administrative Structure

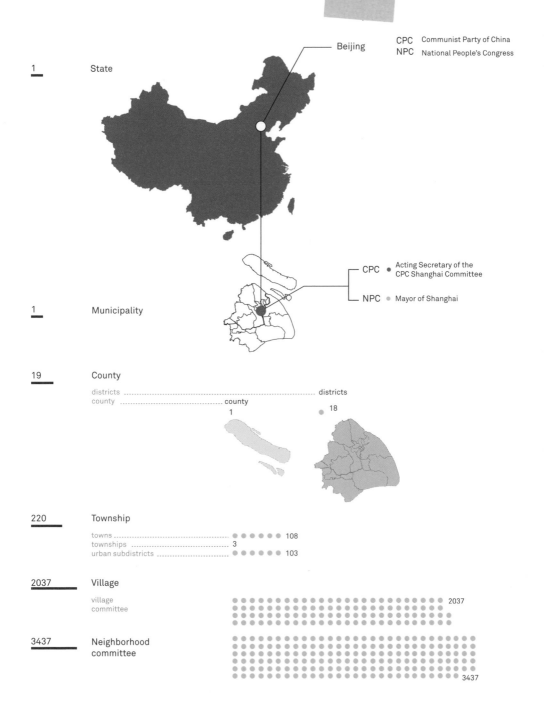

CPC Communist Party of China
NPC National People's Congress

Beijing

1   State

CPC ● Acting Secretary of the
        CPC Shanghai Committee

NPC ● Mayor of Shanghai

1   Municipality

19   County

districts .... districts
county .... county
                                     1   18

220   Township

towns .... ● ● ● ● ● ● 108
townships 3
urban subdistricts .... ● ● ● ● ● ● 103

2037   Village

village
committee   2037

3437   Neighborhood
committee   3437

Source: *Shanghai Statistical Yearbook 2006*. Shanghai Municipal Statistics Bureau.
(Beijing: China Statistics Press, 2006) Table 13.2 Also available online and as a CD-ROM.

● = 20 persons

Buildings by Administrative Division
2005

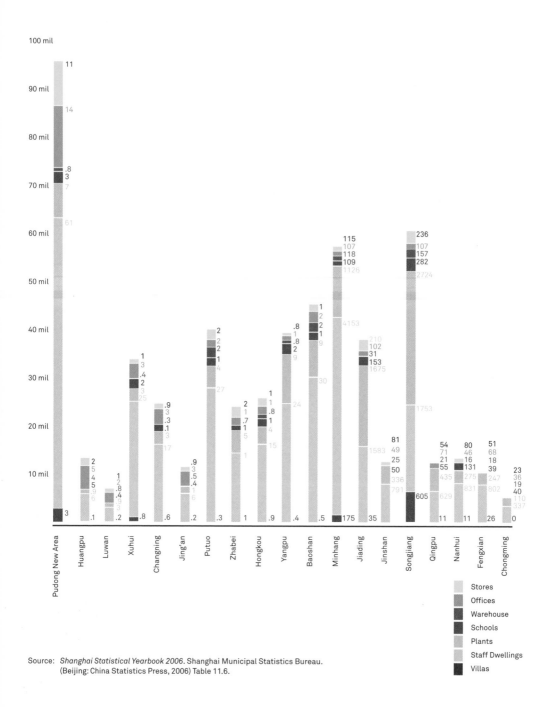

Source: *Shanghai Statistical Yearbook 2006*. Shanghai Municipal Statistics Bureau.
(Beijing: China Statistics Press, 2006) Table 11.6.

Legend:
- Stores
- Offices
- Warehouse
- Schools
- Plants
- Staff Dwellings
- Villas

Building Construction
1978-2005

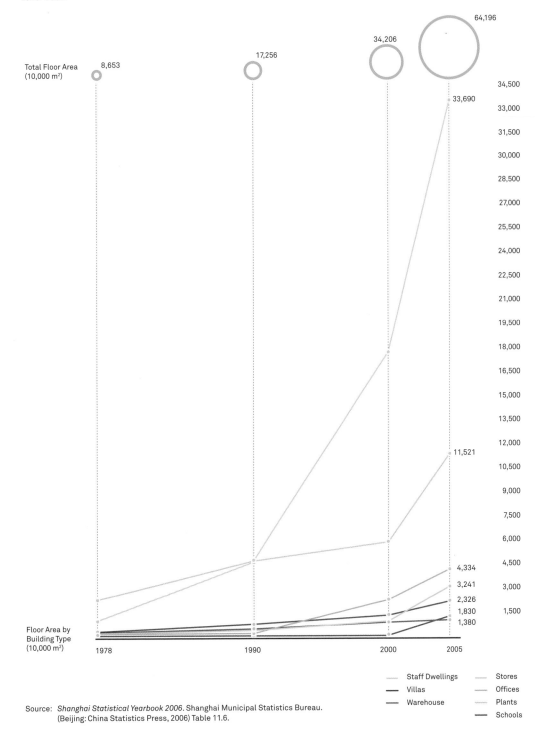

Total Floor Area (10,000 m²)

8,653   17,256   34,206   64,196

34,500
33,690
33,000
31,500
30,000
28,500
27,000
25,500
24,000
22,500
21,000
19,500
18,000
16,500
15,000
13,500
12,000
11,521
10,500
9,000
7,500
6,000
4,500
4,334
3,241
3,000
2,326
1,830
1,500
1,380

Floor Area by Building Type (10,000 m²)

1978   1990   2000   2005

Staff Dwellings — Stores
Villas — Offices
Warehouse — Plants
Schools

Source: *Shanghai Statistical Yearbook 2006*. Shanghai Municipal Statistics Bureau. (Beijing: China Statistics Press, 2006) Table 11.6.

Floor Space of Buildings Over 8 Stories
2005

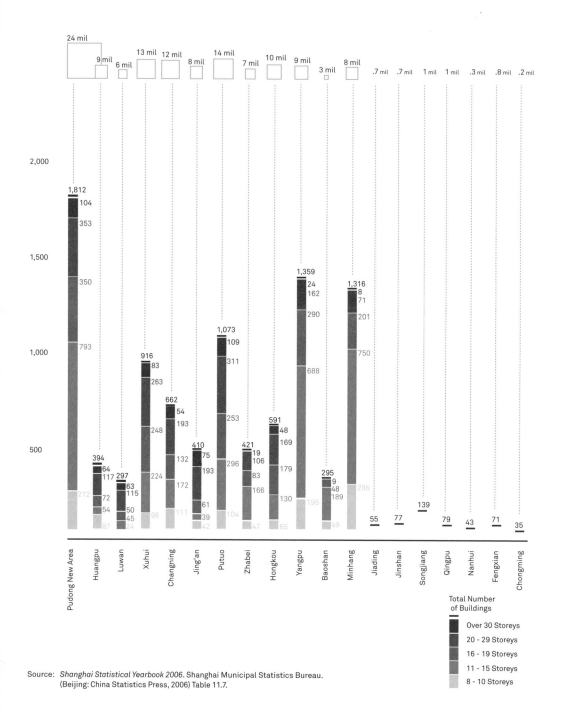

Source: *Shanghai Statistical Yearbook 2006*. Shanghai Municipal Statistics Bureau.
(Beijing: China Statistics Press, 2006) Table 11.7.

Buildable Area
2005

Pudong
1,043 km²
522 km²

Minhang
639 km²
371 km²

Baoshan
479 km²
271 km²

Yangpu
415 km²
61 km²

Putuo
426 km²
55 km²

Xuhui
418 km²
55 km²

Jiading
398 km²
458 km²

Sonjiang
631 km²
605 km²

Nahui
687 km²
687 km²

Hongkou
287 km²
23 km²

Zhabei
257 km²
30 km²

Qingpu
141 km²
676 km²

Fengxian
135 km²
687 km²

Changning
290 km²
38 km²

Chongming
64 km²
1,185 km²

Jinshan
143 km²
586 km²

Huangpu
186 km²
12 km²

Luwan
124 km²
8 km²

Jing'an
149 km²
8 km²

Total Built Area:
6,419 km²

Total Land Area:
6,334 km²

Adminstrative Area

Built Area (km²)

Land Area (km²)

Source: *Shanghai Statistical Yearbook 2006*. Shanghai Municipal Statistics Bureau.
(Beijing: China Statistics Press, 2006) Table 11.3, 11.5.

Land Use
2020

Residential
Transportation
Municipal Utilities
Commercial & Public Facilities
Warehouse
Industrial
Eco-sensitive Area
Green Space

Yangtze River

Huangpu River

Hangzhou Bay

N

0 1 5 10 20 km

Source: *Summary of the Comprehensive Plan of Shanghai (1999-2020)*. Shanghai Urban Planning
Administration Bureau. Shanghai Urban Planning and Design Research Institute.

Transportation
2020

▨ Secondary Road	───
▨ Arterial Road	───
▨ Expressway	───
○ Transfer Hub	
▨ Maglev	───
▨ Metro & Light Rail	───
▨ Metro Alternative	-----
▨ Shanghai Metro	╍╍╍

Yangtze River

Huangpu River

Hangzhou Bay

N

0 1   5   10   20 km

Source: *Summary of the Comprehensive Plan of Shanghai (1999-2020)*. Shanghai Urban Planning
Administration Bureau. Shanghai Urban Planning and Design Research Institute.

Road System
2020

Source: *Summary of the Comprehensive Plan of Shanghai (1999-2020)*. Shanghai Urban Planning
Administration Bureau. Shanghai Urban Planning and Design Research Institute.

Secondary Road

Arterial Road

Expressway

Yangtze River

Huangpu River

Hangzhou Bay

N

0 1 5 10 20 km

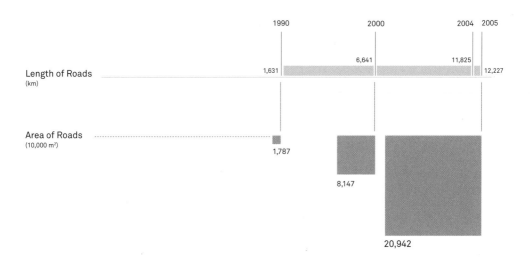

Length of Roads
(km)

Area of Roads
(10,000 m²)

1990   2000   2004 2005

1,631   6,641   11,825   12,227

1,787

8,147

20,942

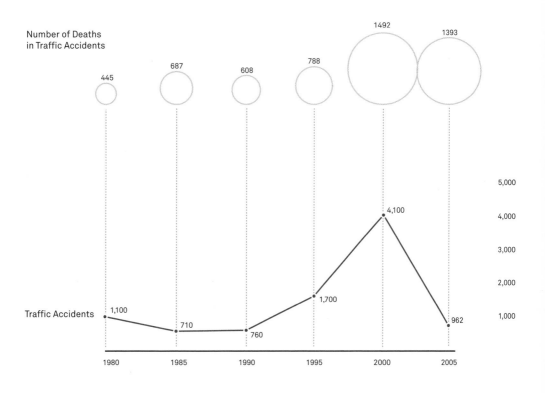

Number of Deaths
in Traffic Accidents

445   687   608   788   1492   1393

5,000

4,000

4,100   3,000

2,000

1,700   1,000

Traffic Accidents

1,100   710   760   962

1980   1985   1990   1995   2000   2005

Source: *Shanghai Statistical Yearbook 2006*. Shanghai Municipal Statistics Bureau.
          (Beijing: China Statistics Press, 2006) Table 11.8, 24.7

Public Transportation
2020

Source: *Summary of the Comprehensive Plan of Shanghai (1999-2020)*. Shanghai Urban Planning
Administration Bureau. Shanghai Urban Planning and Design Research Institute.

Legend:
- ○ Transfer Hub
- Maglev_RT ——————
- Proposed Maglev_RT - - - - -
- Metro & Light Rail ——————
- Metro Alternative ············
- Shanghai Metro ——————

Yangtze River

Huangpu River

Hangzhou Bay

N

0 1 5 10 20 km

Length of Metro Systems

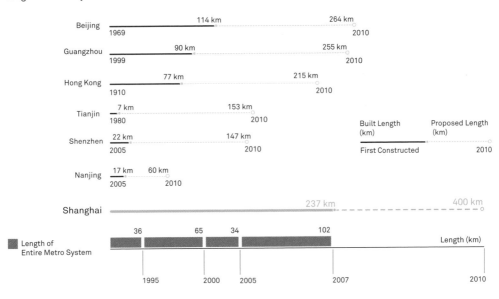

Beijing 1969 — 114 km .... 264 km 2010

Guangzhou 1999 — 90 km .... 255 km 2010

Hong Kong 1910 — 77 km .... 215 km 2010

Tianjin 1980 — 7 km .... 153 km 2010

Shenzhen 2005 — 22 km .... 147 km 2010

Nanjing 2005 — 17 km 60 km 2010

Built Length (km) — Proposed Length (km)
First Constructed — 2010

Shanghai 237 km — 400 km

Length of Entire Metro System

| 36 | 65 | 34 | 102 | Length (km) |

1995   2000   2005   2007   2010

Length of Public Bus Lines

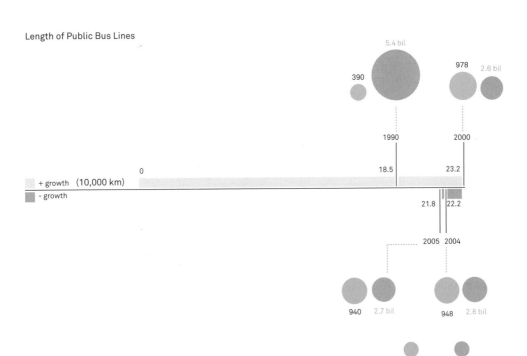

5.4 bil
390
978   2.6 bil

1990   2000

0   18.5   23.2

+ growth (10,000 km)
- growth

21.8 22.2

2005 2004

940 2.7 bil   948 2.8 bil

Number of Bus Lines   Passenger volume (billion persons)

Sources: *Shanghai Statistical Yearbook 2006*. Shanghai Municipal Statistics Bureau.
(Beijing: China Statistics Press, 2006) Table 11.12
Schwandl, Robert. Urban Rail Database. urbanrail.net, http://www.urbanrail.net
(accessed September 30, 2007).
Wikipedia contributors, "List of urban rail systems by length," Wikipedia, The Free Encyclopedia,
http://en.wikipedia.org/w/index.php?title=List_of_urban_rail_systems_by_length&oldid=215684316
(accessed September 30, 2007).

Shanghai Maglev

2001–2007

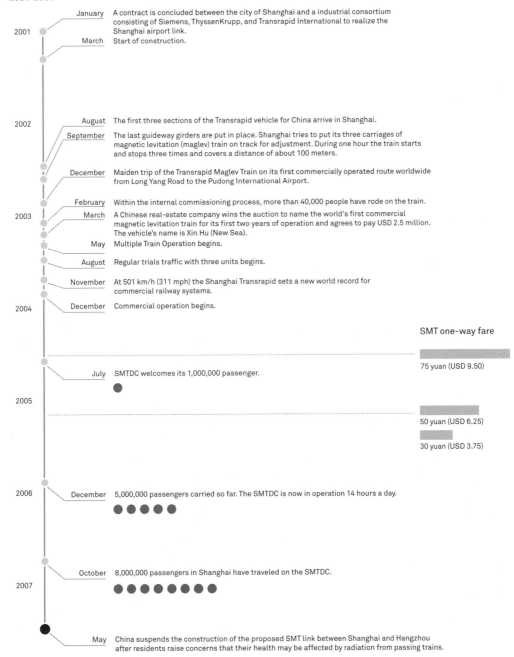

2001

January — A contract is concluded between the city of Shanghai and a industrial consortium consisting of Siemens, ThyssenKrupp, and Transrapid International to realize the Shanghai airport link.

March — Start of construction.

2002

August — The first three sections of the Transrapid vehicle for China arrive in Shanghai.

September — The last guideway girders are put in place. Shanghai tries to put its three carriages of magnetic levitation (maglev) train on track for adjustment. During one hour the train starts and stops three times and covers a distance of about 100 meters.

December — Maiden trip of the Transrapid Maglev Train on its first commercially operated route worldwide from Long Yang Road to the Pudong International Airport.

2003

February — Within the internal commissioning process, more than 40,000 people have rode on the train.

March — A Chinese real-estate company wins the auction to name the world's first commercial magnetic levitation train for its first two years of operation and agrees to pay USD 2.5 million. The vehicle's name is Xin Hu (New Sea).

May — Multiple Train Operation begins.

August — Regular trials traffic with three units begins.

November — At 501 km/h (311 mph) the Shanghai Transrapid sets a new world record for commercial railway systems.

2004

December — Commercial operation begins.

SMT one-way fare

75 yuan (USD 9.50)

50 yuan (USD 6.25)

30 yuan (USD 3.75)

2005

July — SMTDC welcomes its 1,000,000 passenger.

2006

December — 5,000,000 passengers carried so far. The SMTDC is now in operation 14 hours a day.

2007

October — 8,000,000 passengers in Shanghai have traveled on the SMTDC.

May — China suspends the construction of the proposed SMT link between Shanghai and Hangzhou after residents raise concerns that their health may be affected by radiation from passing trains.

Sources: Transrapid International GmbH
http://www.transrapid.de/cgi-tdb/en/basics.prg?session=45d314d348d707c2_194931&a_no=9 (accessed January 10, 2008)
Associated Press, "Shanghai's airport Maglev train offering reduced fares in bid to boost ridership," *International Herald Tribune*. September 7, 2006,
http://www.iht.com/articles/ap/2006/09/07/asia/AS_TRV_China_Airport_Train.php (accessed January 10, 2008).
China Daily, "Shanghai-Hangzhou maglev project suspended" CHINA.ORG.CN, May 26, 2007.
http://www.chinadaily.com.cn/bizchina/2007-05/26/content_880964_2.htm (accessed January 10, 2008).

● = 1 million passengers

Residential Use
2020

Residential

Chongming

Jiading

Baoshan

Yangtze River

Putuo

Zhabei

Hongkou

Huangpu River

Yangpu
Pudong

Huangpu

Luwan

Jing'an

Xuhui

Changing

Minhang

Nanhui

Fengxian

Sonjiang

Jinshan

Qingpu

Hangzhou Bay

N

0 1 5 10 20 km

Sources: *Summary of the Comprehensive Plan of Shanghai (1999-2020)*. Shanghai Urban Planning
Administration Bureau. Shanghai Urban Planning and Design Research Institute.
Shanghai Statistical Yearbook 2006. Shanghai Municipal Statistics Bureau.
(Beijing: China Statistics Press, 2006) Table 18.1, 18.8.

Residential Construction

1985–2005

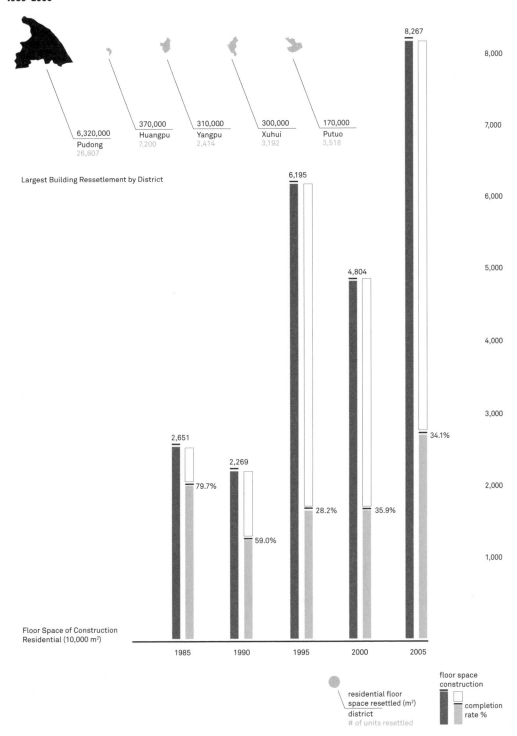

6,320,000
Pudong
26,807

370,000
Huangpu
7,200

310,000
Yangpu
2,414

300,000
Xuhui
3,192

170,000
Putuo
3,518

Largest Building Ressetlement by District

8,267

8,000

6,195

6,000

5,000

4,804

4,000

3,000

2,651

34.1%

2,269

79.7%

59.0%

28.2%

35.9%

2,000

1,000

Floor Space of Construction
Residential (10,000 m²)

1985　　　　1990　　　　1995　　　　2000　　　　2005

residential floor
space resettled (m²)
district
# of units resettled

floor space
construction

completion
rate %

1-9-6-6 Planning Structure

Yangtze River

Huangpu River

Hangzhou Bay

Central City
New City
New Town
Central Villages

N

0 1 5 10 20 km

Sources: *Summary of the Comprehensive Plan of Shanghai (1999-2020)*. Shanghai Urban Planning
Administration Bureau. Shanghai Urban Planning and Design Research Institute.
Beach, Doug, "Shanghai's New Suburbs," National Public Radio, npr.com December 12, 2006
http://www.npr.org/programs/morning/features/2006/dec/shanghai/shanghai_suburbs.html
(accessed November 30, 2007).

Zhu Jia Jiao—Traditional Chinese
Zhu Jia Jiao is an ancient town west of Shanghai that features well-preserved Ming and Qing architecture, with its ancient stone bridges and streets, and network of canals. Ben Wood Studio Shanghai, which designed the popular Xintiandi commercial area in downtown Shanghai, also designed Zhu Jia Jiao's new center: Cambridge Water Town.

Cheng Qiao—Traditional Southern Chinese
Chen Qiao, to be built in the southern Chinese style, is located to the northeast of downtown Shanghai. The German firm Stadbauatelier designed the development. The mainly white and light gray, low buildings are built around canals and have traditional gabled roofs.

An Ting—German
An Ting features German-style buildings designed by Albert Speer, the son of Hitler's favorite architect. The town, located near Shanghai's border with neighboring Jiangsu province, is one of the centers of China's car industry: The German-Chinese joint venture, Shanghai Volkswagen, employs many of its inhabitants. The Shanghai International Circuit, China's first Formula 1 racetrack, is located near the town.

Luo Dian—Swedish
Luo Dian, designed by SWECO FFNS, features Swedish-style buildings. It is an ancient town in Shanghai's northern section, established in the Ming Dynasty more than 700 years ago.

Song Jiang—English
Designed by British firm Atkins, Thames Town is the city center of the new Song Jiang development. This area is partly designed to become a university town, and it is planned for seven universities to move out of Shanghai to Song Jiang in the future.

Pu Jiang—Italian
Italian architect Augusto Cagnardi designed Pu Jiang, the largest of the nine new towns. The town, with Italian-style buildings and canals based on Venice, is located on the east bank of the Huangpu River, a tributary to the Yangtze. Nearly 10 miles from downtown Shanghai, this key location is also five miles from the 2010 World Expo Site. Planners envisage the town housing 80,000 inhabitants.

Feng Cheng—Spanish
Designed by Spanish architect Marcià Codinachs, the 600-year-old coastal fortification of Feng Cheng will be transformed into a Spanish-style township modeled after Barcelona. The town's new residents will mainly be employees of local logistics-equipment companies. Officials hope Feng Cheng's ancient walls and cobblestone lanes will help make the town a new day-trip destination for tourists from Shanghai.

Harbor New Town—European
Harbor New Town is located at the confluence of the Yangtze River and Hangzhou Bay, 31 miles southeast of downtown Shanghai. The development is adjacent to Yangshan International Deep Sea Harbor and Pudong international airport, and officials hope it will be the base for Shanghai's booming logistic business and port industry. Designed by German architect GMP (Gerkan, Marg und Partner), Harbor New Town will be environment-focused, featuring China's largest man-made lake.

Feng Jing—Canadian
Designed by Canadian architecture firm SADA, Feng Jing is a Canadian-style town in southwest Shanghai, with rows of country villas and forests of maple trees.

1-9-6-6 Planning
By 2020, the city's development goals are to preliminarily build Shanghai into one of the world economic, financial, trade and shipping centers,to allocate Shanghai basically as an international economic central metropolis. The 1-9-6-6 Urban Structure outlines the development of 1 Cetnral City, 9 New Cities (+300,000 population each), 60 New Towns (50-100,000 population each), and 600 Central Villages (2,000 population each).

Expo 2010 proposed master plan

World Expo Shanghai 2010

Election
December 3, 2002 at the 132nd general
assembly of the Bureau of International
Expositions (BIE) in Monte Carlo.

Theme
'Better City, Better Life'

Emblem
The emblem, depicting the image of three
people – you, me, him/her – holding
hands together, symbolizes the big family
of mankind.

Duration
May 1-October 31st 2010

Area
5.28 km² is on the waterfront area on
both sides of the Huangpu River, mostly
between Nanpu Bridge and Lupu Bridge.
The eastern part of the site covers
3.93 km² and the western part 1.35 km².

Expected participants
200 nations and international organisa-
tions.

Expected attendance
70 million visitors from home and
abroad.

Cost
25 billion yuan (about 3.01 billion USD),
according to Jiang Yingshi, director of
the Shanghai Municipal Development and
Reform Commission.

Sources:
Bureau of the Shanghai World Expo Coordination.
www.expo2010china.com
People's Daily Online. http://english.people.com.
cn/200311/01/eng20031101_127371.shtml

Expo 2010 site in 2006

Shanghai, along with Rome and Tokyo, is my favorite city in the world. I love it for its juxtaposition of cultures going back more than 150 years and for the dynamic quality this gives the city. In its international enclaves are picturesque suburban mansions of the early 20th century that could easily be on Long Island or the Philadelphia Main Line. There too you can experience the meeting of Nanjing Road, an Asian/Chinese commercial street teeming with pedestrian activity and dynamic signage, and the Bund, a boulevard bordered by European monumental, civic-classical buildings. At the junction of the two sits the Art Deco Peace Hotel with its jazz band in the cocktail lounge where you sip martinis, and its French restaurant par excellence in the penthouse.

Eastern and Western cultures are juxtaposed throughout the city, including the old city, in the southeast, with its famous classic Chinese garden, the Yu Yuan Garden, and in the vast districts beyond, where hundreds of high-rise office and apartment buildings might be considered more Western than Eastern in their scale and symbolism.

Chinese friends tell me that the famous movie *The Last Emperor* correctly represents evolutions within Chinese history in the 20th century. In it we see the cultural evolution in Beijing and in latter-day Shanghai, spanning from an ancient, tradition-bound empire, to a Scott-Fitzgerald era of the 1920s, to Japanese imperial impositions, and then to a strict Communist culture. But in the China Denise Scott Brown and I visited, change is everywhere: commercial and intellectual cultures are booming and, via the cultural juxtapositions of the last 20 years, creativity abounds.

Robert Venturi

We had always wanted to visit Shanghai because of our fascination with its multiculturalism and its particular relevance in our time. We have made three trips there in four years and are working on a project for two high-rise office buildings in the Dalian Road district, for a client who encourages us to develop our ideas on Architecture as Sign.

Shanghai
Denise Scott Brown

In Shanghai today, opportunity seems to vibrate on the streets. It reads on people's faces as they go about their business or walk the river embankment and the commercial sidewalks. And part of the opportunity—and the fun—lies in the city's enormous diversity. In 2003, Robert Venturi and I were invited to China to lecture and consult on campus planning and architecture. We accepted the invitation in order to see the country and to work as architects, but also to indulge our fascination with China's culture and with its centuries of cultural interaction, worldwide.

Chinoiserie in European art and architecture and glimpses of Shanghai Art Deco in the film *The Last Emperor* are examples of the cultural exchanges that fascinate us, but so too is China's ancient history of globalism. In Africa, a trail of traders' beads proves that Arab and African merchants penetrated from the north as far south as the outskirts of Johannesburg, centuries before Europeans arrived at the Cape of Good Hope—but discoveries of shards of Celadon pottery on the South African east coast suggest early relationships with China as well. Archaeologists believe the broken blue-green pieces were used, like the beads, for exchange.

View of the Huangpu River with the pedestrian promenade on the Bund side

Sixteenth-century Chinese engravings of African elephants and giraffes testify further to global connections in a world where not only Europeans made voyages of discovery. Those European venturers who traveled the Chinese Silk Road found themselves part of a multiracial surge of merchants that included Persians, Arabs and Jews who had plied their wares in China from the second century BCE. Xu Xin recounts the story of a meeting between a Jesuit priest and a Jew from Kaifeng in 1605. The Jew had heard that a group of foreigners who believed in one God was building a church, so he initiated contact with people he believed might be Jewish. The priest responded, thinking he was about to discover Christians in China. The confusion that ensued, as the Jesuit tried without success to convince the Jew that the Messiah had indeed arrived in his absence, was indicative of the kind of diversity that had existed in China for centuries.[1]

Shanghai's globalism, however, came later, after the British established a trading post in the city in the 1840s. From that time and until 1949, waves of foreign settlement and growth left their mark on the city. The English and French Concessions and later the International Settlement were places of living and working for foreigners in Shanghai. Organized around the port and the Huangpu River, they served the uses of all expatriate groups and, in the 1930s and '40s, accommodated Chinese and European refugees as well. In 1987 they were the setting for Steven Spielberg's movie, *Empire of the Sun*, filmed on the commercial Bund and in a residential neighborhood where the fictitious English family occupied a home that could have been built, furnished and landscaped in Surrey.

These traces of an earlier multiculturalism that remain today intrigue us, not for what the Chinese learned from the visitors, but for how the people of Shanghai have adapted the inherited Western forms to their own needs and the changing times.

1 — Xu Xin, *The Jews of Kaifeng: History, Culture and Religion* (Jersey City: KTAV Publishing House, 2003).

Robert Venturi + Denise Scott Brown

The Bund is a street of nineteenth- and twentieth-century commercial buildings, strung out along the river, much as banking houses, corporate offices, and hotels would have been at the same time along a European urban river or lakefront, or on and around Fleet Street in London. Today, buildings on the Bund have hardly changed. Just off it, however, they have been acculturated. Former banks, department stores and offices are now densely occupied by Chinese enterprises and draped and decorated to conform to the teeming commercial life of Nanjing Road. There is a spectacular contrast between the gravity of the Bund and the sign-laden vitality of the Road.

Where the two streets meet sits the Peace Hotel. Once the Hotel Cathay, it was the flagship of the Sassoon family: Baghdad-Jewish merchants and financiers who moved, in one century, from robed and turbaned Eastern potentates to English aristocrats and literati.

From its pivotal point on the Bund overlooking the busy industrial and commercial river, the venerable Art Deco-style hotel surveys a diversity of people and activities. Its chief contributions to that diversity are a French restaurant and an Oak Bar, where aged Chinese jazz players perform American swing. That these are at once a survival from pre-Communist times and a vital part of the present scene seems appropriate for China now. The CD *Old Jazz Band. Peace Hotel*, on sale in the bar, lists famous numbers by retranslated titles—"Tea for a couple" and "Laughing brilliantly while weeping inwardly." [2]

From its guest rooms and roof terrace, the Peace Hotel offers views of the crowded river embankment, where tourists and citizens mingle. Shanghai workers do morning exercises there—middle-aged ladies in warm-ups move and sway from sunrise, seemingly without rest, for several hours.

Early photographs show the Bund, the river and on the opposite bank, fragments of decrepit, semi-industrial and semi-rural settlement. But look across the river today and you see fairyland. Pudong is the latest wave of globalism—a latter day "American Concession," perhaps—although Pacific Rim-American is beyond anything in America. Here the high-density skyscraper, its structure and form now universal, has been given a Shanghai air. Until a recent building moratorium, while planners try to think, Shanghai was the home of a majority of the world's heavy construction cranes. Not all were in Pudong. One puzzle for Westerners is why well-off people in Shanghai and other Chinese cities are prepared, even happy, to countenance extremely high-density living. The new housing towers, set cheek by jowl beside each other, seem to form stockades around desirable neighborhoods. In North America and Europe they would be shunned. Here they are quickly rented.

But Pudong is a fantasy from across the river only. Hit the ground on its side and you are in a nightmare. The city below the towers is hostile even to cars, let alone to pedestrians. It would be fascinating to analyze the ground floor patterns of skyscraper Pudong: to map its circulation routes by all modes of transportation, to juxtapose upon these the entry-level plans of all its buildings, and to then seek coherence between the systems of movement and those of access—between going and stopping. A cohesive arrange-

2 — Shanghai: 2002.

ment would relate building entrances to those points in the circulation system where people become pedestrians: transit stops, car drop-offs, parking structure entrances. It would relate main streets to service streets, and then to building service yards and loading bays. Within and from the resulting patterns, civic places of amenity and refuge and various forms of welcome for workers and visitors could be derived.

The Pudong towers raise questions on the use of lighting for beauty and communication. When a building has a rectangle of LED signage slapped across its middle—no matter how large or extensive—this is anti-fantasy. LED technology is, I understand, about to break the bounds of the rectangle. It badly needs to do so if it is to use its capacity for evocation as well as for information. It should be free to swirl, as was the earlier neon, without paying orthogonal respect to architecture.

Our work in China commenced during a phase of spectacular economic development, when outside experts and returning expatriates were called upon to help spur the process of change. Since that time, Chinese architects trained in the West but experienced in their own country, have increasingly assumed the types of responsibilities we were given. Parallel to this shift but less visible have been reversals in the direction of influence: the visiting experts are learning from China.

Bob and I have a long experience of traveling to learn. From our appraisals of Rome and Las Vegas, it could be assumed that we would be intrigued by the signs and symbols of Shanghai (which indeed we are). But we find some equally interesting lessons in the buildings and landscapes of this city. Might aspects of Shanghai's urban morphology be applicable to other countries and cultures today?

As world cities diversify, so developers and planners try to offer various social and income groups a broader range of housing choices in different locations within an urban region. Today's globalism should encourage an international search for new housing prototypes that could be a part of the residential mix. Perhaps the most relevant Shanghai candidates for adoption elsewhere would be the *lilong*. Denser than Levittown or the New Urbanism, but not as dense as high-rise apartment buildings, this housing type emerged from the mews housing of London during the architectural-cultural exchanges of the mid-nineteenth-century. *Lilong* occur within the centers of city blocks where retail activities cannot succeed. Their narrow alleys, lined by small houses, are entered via decorative arches on the main street's commercial frontage. In this way, areas of private living are defined within very public places.

Another import from China could be the scholar's garden. Our guide to these gardens in Shanghai was Luo Xiaowei, a venerated professor of architectural history at Tongji University. They are one of her great interests.[3] Another is United States post World War II architecture. Professor Luo is herself part of the global culture of Shanghai. When she visited our office in Manayunk in 1982, we were amazed that a person from so distant a place should have a deeper understanding of what we stood for than have many American and European scholars.

3 — Jiaji Zhang, Luo Xiaowei, "The Chinese Conception of Space," in *Spazio e Societá/Space & Society 34* (Cambridge, MA: MIT Press, June 1986).

With loving care and amusement Professor Luo demonstrated the principles of the scholar's garden. It is a small landscape crammed into the close quarters of an existing city. Yet despite the intense series of experiences it offers, it seems to escape its limits and to stretch to some distant, invisible place. As I surveyed the enlightened academic's artfully arranged walls and planting that obscured the boundaries of the site, and the serpentine waterway that seemed to disappear on a far journey under a culvert but in fact ended half a meter away, I wondered how these principles might play out in a Western design for a garden in Manhattan.

And I fantasized about coming to Shanghai on a voyage of discovery—in search of new urban prototypes and spending a working vacation in the city, in a spa hotel attached to a scholar's garden. Every morning, after my sauna, I would follow the way of the ancient scholar, down his paths, up his little hill, to his small summer house with a long view, and set myself up in there and do my work.

View of the Oriental Pearl Tower and Pudong from the Jin Mao Tower

Shanghai Urban Planning Exhibition Hall. Renmin Square, Shanghai

Shanghai's Spectacles
Sharon Haar

Urban planning exhibitions are common in China. The Beijing Planning Exhibition Hall sits adjacent to Tiananmen Square, and even Foshan, a "small" city of three million in Guangdong Province, boasts an elaborate model, historical displays, and models of planned developments and buildings. In Shanghai, the Exhibition Hall is part of a quartet of buildings within People's Square. It is joined with the Shanghai Grand Theatre, City Hall, and the Shanghai Museum, suggesting the importance of planning in the culture, politics, and, not least of all, the economy of China as a whole and the city in particular. Like the extensive models and showrooms for new suburban residential developments around the country, the Exhibition Halls' showcase models merge promotion and display. They are not replicas, but idealizations. Historic maps, photographs, models, and tableaus have their place in the halls, but the loss of the physical past of the city—its distinctive building types, communities, and social networks—is hardly sentimentalized. Instead, the past is more phantasmagoria than precedent in models that elaborately boast the potentials of "socialist market economy" as it is plays out in space and time. As such, the halls play a significant role in the interurban competition being played out across the country.

"The spectacle of Shanghai produces a delirium of the visible that erases the difference between old and new," wrote Ackbar Abbas of the complimentarity of the buildings of the Bund and the skyscrapers of Pudong as China entered the twenty-first century.[1] But as early-twentieth and early-twenty-first century globalism mirror one another across the Huangpu River, the Shanghai Urban Planning Exhibition Hall in Renmin Square is the true space of *achronicity*, "where past and present disappear in each other." [2] No less visually spectacular than the Pudong's nighttime skyline—with its dazzling ostentation of lights and electronic images—the city model on display at the top of the building offers an open invitation "for citizens to comprehend the changes in the city and its future planning."[3]

English-language websites for tourists recommend the Shanghai Urban Planning Exhibition Hall as a base for comprehending the city's past (quickly disappearing from the street experience, and illegible through the haze experienced at the top of the Oriental Pearl Tower) and its inexorable growth (witnessed at every corner and at the end of every new highway). In the Hall, one need not just imagine the scope of Shanghai's horizontal and vertical sprawl. It stretches out before you and can be circumnavigated along walkways that serve as a peripheral ring road. Viewing it from above replicates arriving on a plane on a rare clear day. For the foreigner, tourist websites suggest, there is a double opportunity for gazing. In addition to the awe-inspiring size and intricacy of the model (believed to be accurate to 2020) we can take the opportunity to gaze upon the locals who, we are told, visit the hall as much to learn about the future of transportation and sustainability in their city as to discern the viability of their current homes in future development plans (the model is said to contain all existing, in-construction, and approved-for-construction buildings, infrastructure, and developments).

The spectacular models and exhibits of the Shanghai Urban Planning Exhibition Hall are not without historical precedent. They fit into the trajectory of World's Fairs: the modern wares displayed in the Crystal Palace (London, 1851); the modern engineering celebrated in the Eiffel Tower (Paris, 1889); and the Futurama , an image of America twenty years into the future, designed by Norman Bel Geddes for the General Motors Pavilion (New York, 1939). In the case of the Futurama, an enormous pavilion, seated visitors "traveled" around a large-scale model of a rural-suburban-urban landscape linked together by highways and punctuated by cities of modernist skyscrapers. As hallmarks of modernization, urbanization, and later, globalization, World's Fairs and Expositions offer visions of the city of the future, heralding the "society of the spectacle." Guy Debord wrote of the end phase of capitalist accumulation: "In societies where modern conditions of production prevail, all of life presents itself as an immense accumulation of *spectacles*. Everything that was directly lived has moved away into a representation." [4] The Shanghai Urban

1 — Ackbar Abbas, "Play it Again Shanghai: Urban Preservation in the Global Era," in *Shanghai Reflections. Architecture, Urbanism, and the Search for an Alternative Modernity* (New York: Princeton Architectural Press, 2002), 51.
2 — Ackbar Abbas, "Building on Disappearance: Hong Kong architecture and colonial space," *The Cultural Studies Reader*, 2nd ed. (NewYork: Routledge, 2003), 156.
3 — *Beijing Shanghai Architecture Guide, Architecture and Urbanism Special Issue* (Tokyo: A+U Publishing Co., Ltd., 2005), 127.
4 — Guy Debord, *Society of the Spectacle* (Detroit: Black & Red, 1970), 1.

Planning Exhibition Hall imagines a vision of the future determined by the odd alliance of communism and capitalism. To a tourist, it is a spectacle of propaganda on par with the spectacle of capitalism that is Pudong by night.

The giant model housed in the Shanghai Urban Planning Exhibition Hall recalls the 2743 square meter Panorama of the City of New York at the 1964 New York World's Fair, a celebration of the urban planner Robert Moses's attempt to accomplish Geddes's future vision. Like the Futurama, the Panorama was significant not just for its scale, but also for the spectacular experience of traveling by car around its perimeter. Unlike its predecessor, however, it was not futuristic but based on the facts of a real city at a particular historical moment—New York City—and the new buildings and highways that were included anticipated the city's future growth by only one year. As the centerpiece of the New York City Pavilion, the Panorama initially served similarly multifaceted purposes as contemporary Chinese planning exhibitions. It too was surrounded by models and images of the city's past. Indeed, Moses was a strong believer in the persuasive power of large-scale models and frequently used them to promote his projects for the state and city.[5] The Panorama was intended to illustrate the culmination of a 300-year trajectory (starting with the takeover of New Amsterdam by the British in 1664) but, as Christine Boyer has noted, its greater purpose was to acknowledge and record Moses's own impact on the city.[6] It was only updated until 1972, the end of Moses's fifty-year career as New York's "Power Broker:" a position he held by virtue of his simultaneous control of multiple state and city planning authorities. Although it was also promoted as a planning tool for visualizing large-scale planning possibilities, it was rarely used for this purpose and certainly was not intended to promote public participation in design or planning decisions. Even as Moses was preparing for the 1964 World's Fair, his position as New York City's sole master planner was under attack, most notably by community organizations under the leadership of Jane Jacobs. These citizens fought to preserve their neighborhoods, slated for demolition to make way for the Lower Manhattan Expressway. By the 1970s it was no longer possible to carry out significant infrastructure or building projects in New York City without community input and approval—and the Panorama became a historical artifact as part of the Queens Museum. (It was last updated in 1995, and is scheduled for an update in the near future.) Perhaps symbolizing the speed and ambition of Shanghainese urban development, the Shanghai Urban Planning Exhibition Hall already exists as a foreshadowing of Expo 2010 to be housed along the Haungpu River with the motto "Better City, Better Life." Scheduled to open simultaneously with the Exposition will be the first stage of a model community—the Dongtan Eco-City on Chongming Island—which is hoped to be the sustainable answer to the unsustainable growth of Shanghai proper. Here, the future vision of the World's Fairs will reach its apotheosis.

5 — Marc H. Miller, *The Panorama of New York City: A History of the World's Largest Scale Model* (New York: Queens County Art and Cultural Center, 1990).
6 — M. Christine Boyer, "The Panorama of New York City: A Paradoxical View," in Patricia C. Phillips, ed. *City Speculations* (New York: Princeton Architectural Press, 1996), 17.

Sharon Haar

Dongtan combines the vision of the modernist planner Moses with that of the American visionary Walt Disney, whose proposal for EPCOT (Experimental Prototype Community of Tomorrow) in 1966 was derived from his experience with the pavilions of the 1964 World's Fair. Disney's technological city was to be the centerpiece of his "Disney World" project in central Florida. Ultimately, what was to be a living city became just one of the many Disney theme parks—a continuous World's Fair—and in the 1990s the New Urbanist residential community recalling historic town planning principles called Celebration was built in its stead. Whether the projects on Chongming Island will become self-sustaining communities or EPCOT-like prototypes will remain unclear for many years.

Viewing the model of Shanghai through the lens of the Panorama of the City of New York recalls the spectacle's origin in political, social, and economic forces,and calls into question the agency of the city's citizens in forming their own environments. At what point will the Shanghainese—using the exhibition hall to apprehend the fate of their neighborhoods—begin to organize for a participatory planning and development process along lines initiated by Jacobs. Debord stated: "The spectacle is not a collection of images, but a social relation among people, mediated by images."[7] Does the urban model really aid in the comprehension of the city, or does it further alienate viewers from the actual spatial and temporal transformations being made in their name. In New York City, one can leave the Queens Museum of Art—where the Panorama is still housed—and note that the skyline will always be several steps ahead of its replica. In Shanghai, the exhibition and the skyline vie for accuracy. The only known quantity is that the city one sees entering the hall will not be same upon leaving it.

View of the Panorama
at the NY World's Fair of 1964.
New York City

7 — Debord, *Society of the Spectacle*, 4.

Modern
Monumentality.
Century Avenue,
Shanghai

Urbanizing China
Peter G. Rowe

Since its historic opening to the outside world and partial reform under Deng Xiaoping
in 1978, China is at something of a mid-point in its likely current round of urbanization.
Statistically, in 1979 the proportion of the nation's population in urban settlements,
either in the form of cities or designated towns, was 17.9 percent. This rose to 40.5 percent in 2003 and at an accelerated rate from the late 1990s onwards.[1] Over this period
some 350 million additional people found themselves in urban areas; partially through
natural growth, although China's birthrate had declined; partially, if not primarily, through
migration to designated urban areas; and partially through redefinition of how urban
populations were defined. The magnitude of urbanization between 1978 and the present
is largely unprecedented, with the emergence of something like 468 new cities, 18,000
new designated towns and the accommodation of over half a billion people. Moreover,
these magnitudes will almost certainly continue to grow, with the addition of some 300

1 — All national-level data cited here, except as otherwise noted, are drawn from National Bureau of Statistics
of China, *Cities in China: 1949-1998* (Beijing: Xinhua Press, 1999); National Bureau of Statistics of China, *Urban
Statistical Year Book of China*, 1999-2003 (Beijing: China Statistics Press, 2000-2004).

million urban dwellers over the next 25 years or so, and as many as 500 million by mid-century, or to a point where the urban proportion of total population probably becomes asymptotic at around 60 percent.[2]

Over the previous 25-year period China has demonstrated a reasonable capacity to guide the massive urban influx and a rising level of sophistication in many of the urban projects that have been produced. Infrastructure development, for instance, has been strong. In Shanghai the first subway transit line was completed in 1995, with three lines, totaling about 80 kilometers in length, completed by 2003. A further 17 lines are likely to be installed by around 2020, totaling somewhere between 200 and 540 kilometers of service, depending on the rate of construction.[3] Large-scale public and especially State-sponsored projects have certainly caught the attention of international audiences for their contemporary verve, with the likes of the CCTV complex by Rem Koolhaas, the Olympic Stadium by Herzog and de Meuron, the Shanghai Airport by Paul Andreu and the National Grand Theater in Beijing by the same architect, to name but a few. Attention to public-open space amenity is also clearly on display in the recent "greening" of Shanghai, as well as some other cities, and the reconstitution of once moribund "design institutes," alongside smaller private architectural and planning firms, appears to be having a positive impact on the projects that are being produced.

The Matter of Scale

As China moves further into its present round of urbanization and modernization much is frequently made about the sheer size and scope of the enterprise. It is often said that cities have reached unprecedented sizes and continue to grow. Property transactions mostly occur at the scale of vast tracts and superblocks, with a corresponding influence on the grain and texture of city making. So-called 'megaprojects' are more the rule than the exception and high density is commonplace. Everywhere, or so it seems in urbanizing China, vastness of scale is an issue. To be sure, a massive amount of urbanization has taken place recently in China and seems likely to continue. From the national statistical perspective of designated towns and cities, however, China today has relatively few large cities on a per-capita basis by international experiences, with around 50 within official definitions of a million or more inhabitants. This compares to the United States, for instance, with roughly the same number of metropolitan statistical areas but with less than one quarter of the overall population.[4] To date, none of China's cities figure among the extreme megalopolises of the world. The populations of the nation's three largest cities—Shanghai, Beijing and Tianjin at around thirteen million, twelve million and ten million inhabitants respectively—are nowhere near as large as Tokyo at about thirty-two million, Mexico City and Sao Paolo at around nineteen million each, and New York and Mumbai at close to seventeen million inhabitants each. Depending upon the statistical reference, today Shanghai ranks 10th, Beijing 14th, Tianjin 21st, Hong Kong 28th, Wuhan 38th and Chonqing 40th among the world's largest cities by population.[5]

2 — Rowe, Peter G., *East Asia Modern: Shaping the Contemporary City* (London: Reaktion Press, 2005), 193-194.
3 — Kuan, Seng and Peter G. Rowe, eds., *Shanghai: Architecture and Urbanism for Modern China* (New York: Prestel, 2004).
4 — U.S. Census Bureau, 2000.
5 — *The Economist Pocket World in Figures, 2005 Edition* (London: Profile Books, 2005), 22-23.

Where China's recent urban development really has become extraordinary is among peripheral circumstances and the quickly evolving urban conurbations that have engulfed (or are beginning to engulf) already well-established cities and towns. Moreover, this is where China appears to be struggling most with large-tract developments, ill-considered consolidation of cities and towns, a lack of sufficient planning and design precedents and only a small modicum of guidelines and controls, amid a myriad of local compromises and more than occasional resistance. One place, among others, where these phenomena are occurring is in the Changjiang Delta region. Extending some 350 kilometers in from China's east coast and embracing Jiangsu and Zhejiang Provinces, together with the greater Shanghai administrative area, and including sizeable cities like Shanghai, Nanjing, Wuxi, Suzhou, Hangzhou and Ningbo, the region has a population of some sixty-seven million inhabitants, 53 percent of whom are classified as urban dwellers, well ahead of the national trend.[6] Between 1964 and 1989 the whole region served as a magnet, including for returnees from the earlier sending-down policy in 1976. Then, between 1989 and 1993, the dominant destination for immigration and intra-regional migration was the center of the region, in the neighborhood of Lake Tai, followed, between 1993 and 1998, by all the large cities, of which ten presently have populations in excess of one million inhabitants. Between 1998 and the present, this latter trend has continued plus population expansion of smaller cities in the ambit of large-scale urban areas, like Shanghai, especially given the recent decentralization of larger cities into surrounding areas. In short, what transpired was a staged process, the nascent phase of which was a boom in *in situ* urban settlements, followed by congregation of population in larger urban settlements where agglomeration afforded apparent economic, service and environmental advantages, and then decentralization of larger cities into their peripheries, alongside of growth of smaller existing towns within the mega-urban areas—overall, effectively a bi-polar distributional phenomenon.

Greening of Shanghai.
Century Park,
Shanghai

6 — Provincial-level data are drawn from: National Bureau of Statistics of China, *Statistical Yearbooks for Cities* (Beijing: China Statistics Press, relevant years); *Urban Development Reports of Provinces*. Provincial Statistical Bureaus, relevant years.

Peter G. Rowe

The spatial upshot of this transitional process has been the pronounced emergence of four urban forms within the region.[7] The first is independent urban expansion, occurring mainly in the north and west of the region. The second is the formation of an urban corridor, particularly along the Shanghai-Nanjing expressway, encompassing Suzhou, Wuxi and Changzhou. The third is centralization of urban areas through consolidation as happened, for example, in Zhanjiagang beside the Changjiang River. The fourth—and what may be the most pertinent for the conversation in this collection—is metropolitan expansion of very large urban areas, like Shanghai, which first attracted population and then expanded outward, embracing satellite and other communities in their steady growth. Among the four, the form that is most conspicuous and problematic in terms of scale is the corridor conurbation from Suzhou through Wuxi to Changzhou. There, the combined designated city populations reach 6.5 million inhabitants, to which can be added another equal or greater amount to convey a more accurate depiction of urban contiguity with surrounding, separately-designated urban settlements. To a somewhat lesser extent the same observation can be made of Nanjing and neighboring or growth-path oriented Yangzhou and Zhenjiang, with combined city, let alone urban conurbation populations, of 5.9 million inhabitants.

National-level designations obscure the emergence of truly mega-metropolitan or regional urban concentrations, all weighing in at well over ten million inhabitants and something like half the regional population in total. It is precisely in these circumstances where the real scale effects of contemporary Chinese urbanization are now most present, even if to many they are, as it were, 'out of sight' and 'out of mind.'

Sprawling Peripheral
Development.
Changjiang Delta
region

7 — Zhu Bing, *Urbanization, Spatial Configuration and Regional Management: The Case of the Changjiang Delta Region, China.* Unpublished Doctoral Dissertation, Graduate School of Design, Harvard University, May 2006.

Disaggregating
the Global Economy: Shanghai
Saskia Sassen

The vast new economic topography that is being implemented through electronic space is one moment—one fragment—of an even vaster economic chain that is in good part embedded in non-electronic spaces. There is no fully dematerialized firm or industry. Even the most advanced information industries, such as finance, are installed only partly in electronic space; this also holds for industries that make digital products such as software. In the case of the most complex and high-risk economic activities, their growing digitization has not eliminated their need for major international business and financial centers and all the material resources they concentrate—from state of the art telematics infrastructure to brain talent. In good part, Shanghai's rapid ascent is rooted in these systemic trends that cut across borders and across political and market regimes.[1]

1 — For empirical details about the various issues discussed here see Saskia Sassen, *Cities in a World Economy: Third Edition* (Thousand Oakes: Sage, 2006) and *The Global City*, 2nd ed. (Princeton, Princeton University Press 2001).

Intercity Geographies

Globalization can be deconstructed in terms of the strategic sites where global processes and the linkages that bind them materialize. Among these sites are export-processing zones, offshore banking centers and on a far more complex level, global cities. Together these sites generate a specific geography of globalization and make it clear that globalization is not a planetary event nor does it resemble an expanding oil slick. It is a lumpy geography, and one that has changed over the last few centuries and the last few decades, incorporating diverse types of sites across time and space. Mines, plantations, and merchant markets have been sites in the world economy for millennia. And so have cities.

To get at the question of cities and the global economy, it helps to specify the multiple global circuits through which cities are connecting across borders. Particular networks connect particular groups of cities. This allows us to recover details about the diverse roles of cities in the global economy. Some of these inter-city geographies are thick and highly visible—the flows of professionals, tourists, artists, and migrants among specific groups of cities. Others are thin and barely visible—the highly specialized electronic financial trading networks that connect particular cities depending on the type of instrument involved. A bit thicker are the global commodity chains for diverse products that run from exporting hubs to importing hubs.

These circuits are multidirectional and crisscross the world, feeding into inter-city geographies with both expected and unexpected strategic nodes. For instance, if we consider the leading global markets for trading financial instruments on commodities, we see that New York dominates coffee and London dominates platinum, but Shanghai, a far less powerful financial center, now dominates copper. Cities located on global circuits, whether few or many, become part of distinct and often highly specialized inter-city geographies.

New York and London are clearly part of a global geography of growing numbers and diversity of circuits. They are part of the most powerful global inter-city networks—binding them to Tokyo, Paris, Frankfurt, Zurich, Amsterdam, Toronto, Los Angeles, Sydney, Hong Kong, among others. But this global geography now also includes cities such as Mumbai, Shanghai, Bangkok, Taipei, São Paulo, Mexico City, and Johannesburg.

Shanghai is at the intersection of major global manufacturing, trading and real estate development circuits. It has not yet developed the concentrated level of networked transactions among advanced service firms that exist in New York or London or Hong Kong. However, it is evident that Shanghai is moving in this direction as its overall service sector continues to expand relative to manufacturing[2]. Shanghai is now China's top corporate headquarters city, especially in research and development; Beijing is a close second. Fifty-five multinational companies set up regional headquarters in Shanghai after 2003, leading to increased membership in the city's American Chamber of Commerce. There is an average annual addition of 30 multinationals' R&D centers in Shanghai since

---

2 — See Xiangming Chen, ed., *Shanghai Rising: Global Impact, State Power, and Local Transformations in the World's Most Dynamic and Rapidly Globalizing Mega-City* (Minneapolis: University of Minnesota Press, 2007); Table 1.

2002. This is likely to be partly due to a lack of alternative and competitive locations in China. Unlike other global cities, Shanghai's rise as a top headquarters city has not led to its disconnection from the regional hinterland.

A focus on the presence of translocal chains of operations helps us situate the specifics of a city, a metropolitan area, or an urban region in a far broader systemic dynamic—one that might include both points of sharp agglomeration and of sharp dispersal. Agglomerations can vary sharply in their content and corresponding spatial form, as is evident in the different architectures of density across London's financial center, Mexico City's Santa Fe office district, and Shanghai's Pudong development. Shanghai is both a space for dispersing operations for non-Chinese financial and manufacturing firms, and a space for agglomerating headquarter functions of Chinese firms.

The rapid growth of affiliates illustrates the dynamic of simultaneous geographic dispersal and concentration of the operation of firms [3]. By 1999, firms had well over a half-million affiliates outside their home countries, accounting for USD 11 trillion in sales (a very significant figure if we consider that global trade stood at USD 8 trillion) By 2003, the number of affiliates had doubled—reaching almost a million—and it continued to grow in 2006 [4]. Firms with large numbers of geographically dispersed factories and service outlets face massive new needs for central coordination and servicing This is especially the case when their affiliates involve foreign countries with different legal and accounting systems such as China, which attracted the largest number of foreign affiliates by 2003 [5]. This trend is consistent with the growing number of multinationals setting up their China or Asian regional headquarter offices in Shanghai [6].

Finally, the global capital market is also a translocal chain of operations, with stock markets and financial centers key nodes. The late 1980s and early 1990s saw the addition of markets such as Buenos Aires, São Paulo, Mexico City, Bangkok, Taipei, Moscow, and growing numbers of nonnational firms listed in most of these markets. Shanghai entered the world of financial exchanges in the early 1990s. The total volume of traded stocks on the Shanghai Stock Exchange rose from USD 100 million in 1991 to USD 26 billion in 2003 [7], although its tiny share of global market capitalization dropped from 2002 to 2004. While much was said about Shanghai replacing Hong Kong as China's leading financial center, it is now clear that Shanghai has emerged as a predominantly national market, and that Hong Kong remains a major international exchange. Hong Kong has also drawn most lucrative listings of China's domestic companies, which have turned their backs on Shanghai's sluggish capital markets. However, the Shanghai Stock Market came to life in 2006, rising 130 percent in total traded value and 250 percent in new accounts for the year, which prompted the central government and its affiliated analysts to warn against the market overheating.

3 — See Sassen, *Cities in a World Economy* for a detailed empirical elaboration.
4 — See Table 1.
5 — See Sassen, *Cities in a World Economy*. See information on page 136.
6 — See Chen, *Shanghai Rising*.
7 — Shanghai Statistical Bureau, *Shanghai Statistical Yearbook* (Beijing: China Statistics Press, 2004), 220.

The Urban Footprint of Global Capital

Once we introduce place into analyses of the global economy—particularly as these are constituted in major cities rather than on a coffee plantation—we can begin to see the multiplicity of economies and work cultures in which the global information economy is embedded. Even the most global and advanced firms and financial exchanges need cleaners, truckers and secretaries. This brings the neighborhoods where the workers live—whether high income professionals or migrant workers—into the picture. The construction workers in downtown Shanghai and the cleaners on Wall Street belong to advanced economic sectors, and we miss much of this when we focus on hypermobile electronic financial networks or on global commodity markets alone.

What feeds this expanding urban footprint of global capital (including its most-electronic components) is the fact that global markets and global firms need central places where the most complex work of globalization gets done. Also, firms that can function in electronic networks need a vast physical infrastructure for connectivity—the capacity for global communication is different from the material conditions that make this possible. Focusing on cities allows us to specify a geography of strategic places at the global scale, places bound to each other by the dynamics of economic globalization. It amounts to a new geography of centrality. Together the cities that constitute this geography function as a socio-technical infrastructure for a new global political economy, but also for new cultural and social spaces.

Global cities contain both geographies of centrality and marginality. They may be less visible in Shanghai than in New York City and Johannesburg, but they are there. Downtowns and business centers receive massive investments in real estate and telecommunications, Shanghai being the most extreme example. The new "centers" created at the edge of the city come in close second, notably Johannesburg's Santown and Mexico City's Santa Fe. At the same time, low-income urban and metropolitan areas are starved for resources, with the ghettos in New York City's outer boroughs and the many shanties in Mexico City being two brutal instances.

These spatial outcomes are partly fed by the socio-economic dynamics that produce an extremely highly paid professional stratum of workers and firms as well as an extremely lowly paid and unprotected stratum of marginally surviving, often informal, firms and workers. What distinguishes the current global urban era is that a good share of both types of workers and firms are part of the new advanced urban economy. Financial services produce superprofits while industrial services barely survive—yet both are an intrinsic part of the new urban economy. Add to this that many medium-skilled workers are witnessing their conditions for survival sink, and a stark picture emerges of inequalities often obscured by the highly visible, sharp expansion of luxury spaces for offices, residences and commerce in all of these cities. Inward migrations from overseas or a country's interior are evident in all of them, as well. The picture may be less visible in Shanghai to the Western eye, beyond the evidently foreign workforce, but it exists in the millions of migrants from all corners of China and its many old nations.

Increased socioeconomic inequality was evident in Shanghai during its period of high growth. For instance, Shanghai's Gini index, a measure of income inequality in which 0.0 represents equality and 1.0 represents inequality, rose from .37 in 1994 to .45 in 2001. This increased inequality in Shanghai results from its own specific conditions, partly fed by the bifurcation of the service sector into high-profit and very low-profit services, and partly by a vast low-wage manufacturing and construction boom. Some of this larger income disparity is also the result of the growing informal economy, which absorbs a large number of laid off state-sector factory workers into low-paying service jobs.[8]

Spaces of Centrality in a Global Digital Age

Cities have historically provided national economies, polities and societies with something we can think of as centrality. In terms of their economic function, they provide agglomeration economies, massive concentrations of information on the latest developments and a marketplace. In principle, the new information and communication technologies (ICTs) have the technical capacities to alter—and indeed eliminate—the role of centrality and hence of cities as key economic spaces.

Even as the central business district in major international business hubs remains a strategic site for the leading industries, it is one profoundly reconfigured by technological and economic change[9] and by long-term inward migrations[10]. Further, there are often sharp differences in the patterns assumed by this reconfiguring of the central city in different parts of the world.[11]

The center can extend into a metropolitan area in the form of a grid of nodes of intense business activity, a pattern illustrated by recent developments in cities as diverse as Buenos Aires, Paris, or Shanghai. One might ask whether a spatial organization characterized by dense strategic nodes spread over a broader region does or does not constitute a new form of organizing the territory of the "center," rather than, as in the more conventional view, an instance of suburbanization or geographic dispersal. Insofar as these various nodes are articulated through digital networks and state-of-the-art conventional transport, they can represent a new geographic correlate of the most advanced type of "center." The places that fall outside this new high-connectivity grid, however, remain suburban or may become peripheralized.

8 — Chen, *Shanghai Rising*.

9 — For general background see Susan Fainstein, *The City Builders: Property Development in New York and London, 1980–2000*, 2nd ed. (Lawrence, University Press of Kansas, 2001).

10 — See Michael Laguerre, *The Global Ethnopolis: Chinatown, Japantown and Manilatown in American Society* (London: Macmillion, 2000).

11 — Ricky Burdett, ed., *Cities: People, Society, Architecture* (New York: Rizzoli, 2006); Ricky Burdett and Deyan Sudjic, eds., *The Endless City* (New York: Phaidon, 2008).

This regional grid of nodes represents, in my analysis, a reconstitution of the concept of region, one not based on narrowly geographic or merely administrative boundaries, but on the character of activities and the pertinent infrastructures[12]. Such a partly digital regional grid is likely to be embedded in conventional forms of communications and transport infrastructures, notably mobile phone and Internet networks, as well as rapid rail and highways connecting to airports. In the case of Shanghai, while the build-up of more conventional transport and telecommunications infrastructures such as highways and mobile phones has been rapid, more sophisticated service infrastructures like airport logistics and e-commerce remain lacking.

As illustrated by Shanghai and the surrounding Yangtze River Delta region, there are novel ways in which global cities become articulated with new kinds of regional economies. This is often linked to the development of new types of manufacturing, and sometimes linked to older industrial histories, as is evident in cities as diverse as Chicago, Shanghai and São Paulo. Their pasts as heavy manufacturing regions matters, but not simply as continuations of these older histories.

12 — See for example Regional Plan Association, *Economic Megaregions* (Princeton: Policy Research Institute for the Region, Woodrow Wilson School of Public and International Affairs,Princeton University, 2007).

Economic **Transformation**

World's Busiest Cargo and Container Ports
2005

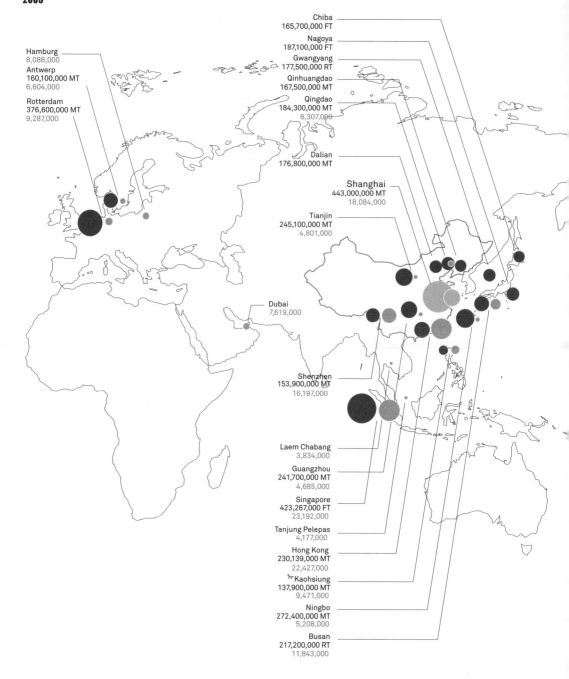

Hamburg
8,088,000
Antwerp
160,100,000 MT
6,604,000
Rotterdam
376,600,000 MT
9,287,000

Chiba
165,700,000 FT
Nagoya
187,100,000 FT
Gwangyang
177,500,000 RT
Qinhuangdao
167,500,000 MT
Qingdao
184,300,000 MT
6,307,000

Dalian
176,800,000 MT

Shanghai
443,000,000 MT
18,084,000

Tianjin
245,100,000 MT
4,801,000

Dubai
7,619,000

Shenzhen
153,900,000 MT
16,197,000

Laem Chabang
3,834,000

Guangzhou
241,700,000 MT
4,685,000

Singapore
423,267,000 FT
23,192,000

Tanjung Pelepas
4,177,000

Hong Kong
230,139,000 MT
22,427,000

Kaohsiung
137,900,000 MT
9,471,000

Ningbo
272,400,000 MT
5,208,000

Busan
217,200,000 RT
11,843,000

Source: American Association of Port Authorities, "World Port Rankings 2005,"
AAPA, American Association of Port Authorities (accessed December 15, 2006)

New York
138,014,000 MT
4,785,000

Los Angeles
7,485,000

Long Beach
6,710,000

Houston
192,023,000 MT

South Louisiana
192,549,000 MT

Total Mass of Actual Cargo:
Metric Tons, Freight Tons, or Revenue Tons

port city
cargo tonnage
container traffic

World Busiest Cargo Traffic
2005

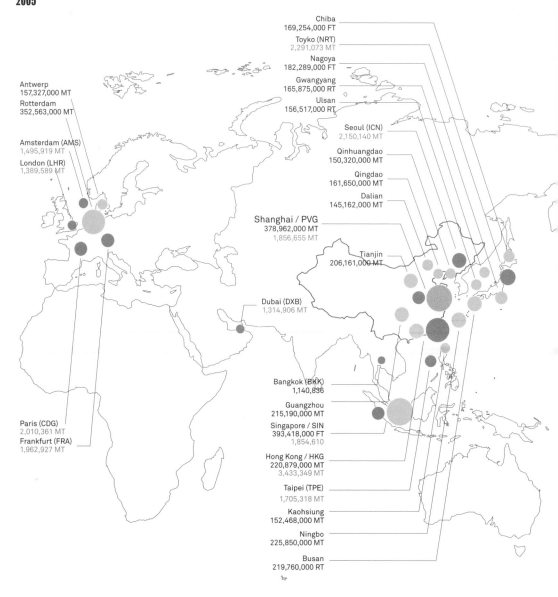

Chiba
169,254,000 FT

Toyko (NRT)
2,291,073 MT

Nagoya
182,289,000 FT

Gwangyang
165,875,000 RT

Ulsan
156,517,000 RT

Seoul (ICN)
2,150,140 MT

Qinhuangdao
150,320,000 MT

Qingdao
161,650,000 MT

Dalian
145,162,000 MT

Shanghai / PVG
378,962,000 MT
1,856,655 MT

Tianjin
206,161,000 MT

Antwerp
157,327,000 MT

Rotterdam
352,563,000 MT

Amsterdam (AMS)
1,495,919 MT

London (LHR)
1,389,589 MT

Dubai (DXB)
1,314,906 MT

Bangkok (BKK)
1,140,836

Guangzhou
215,190,000 MT

Singapore / SIN
393,418,000 FT
1,854,610

Hong Kong / HKG
220,879,000 MT
3,433,349 MT

Taipei (TPE)
1,705,318 MT

Kaohsiung
152,468,000 MT

Ningbo
225,850,000 MT

Busan
219,760,000 RT

Paris (CDG)
2,010,361 MT

Frankfurt (FRA)
1,962,927 MT

Sources: American Association of Port Authorities, "World Port Rankings 2005,"
AAPA, American Association of Port Authorities (accessed December 15, 2006).
Airports Council International, "Cargo Traffic 2005 Final," ACI, Airports Council International
http://www.aci.aero/cda (accessed July 30, 2007).

Anchorage (ANC)†
2,553,937 MT

Chicago (ORD)
1,546,156 MT

Indianapolis (IND)
985,457 MT

New York / JFK
138,328,000 MT
1,660,717 MT

Louisville (SDF)
1,815,155 MT

Memphis (MEM)
3,598,500 MT

Miami (MIA)
1,754,633 MT

South Louisiana
203,517,000 MT

Los Angeles (LAX)
1,938,430 MT

Houston
183,289,000 MT

†ANC data includes transit freight
Total Cargo: either in Metric Tons, Freight Tons, of Revenue Tons
Total Cargo: loaded and unloaded freight and mail in Metric Tons

port city / airport
ship cargo traffic
air cargo traffic

World Busiest Passenger and Movement Airports

2005

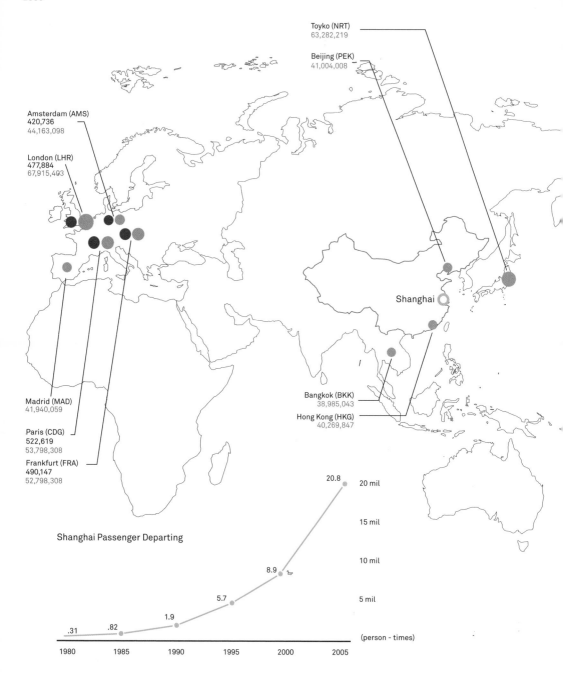

Toyko (NRT)
63,282,219

Beijing (PEK)
41,004,008

Amsterdam (AMS)
420,736
44,163,098

London (LHR)
477,884
67,915,403

Madrid (MAD)
41,940,059

Paris (CDG)
522,619
53,798,308

Frankfurt (FRA)
490,147
52,798,308

Shanghai

Bangkok (BKK)
38,985,043

Hong Kong (HKG)
40,269,847

Shanghai Passenger Departing

20.8 — 20 mil

— 15 mil

8.9 — 10 mil

5.7 — 5 mil

.31   .82   1.9

(person - times)

1980   1985   1990   1995   2000   2005

Sources: *Shanghai Statistical Yearbook 2006*. Shanghai Municipal Statistics Bureau.
(Beijing: China Statistics Press, 2006) Table 15.3.
Airports Council International, "Traffic Movements 2005 Final," "Passenger Traffic 2005 Final,"
ACI, Airports Council International http://www.aci.aero/cda (accessed July 30, 2007).

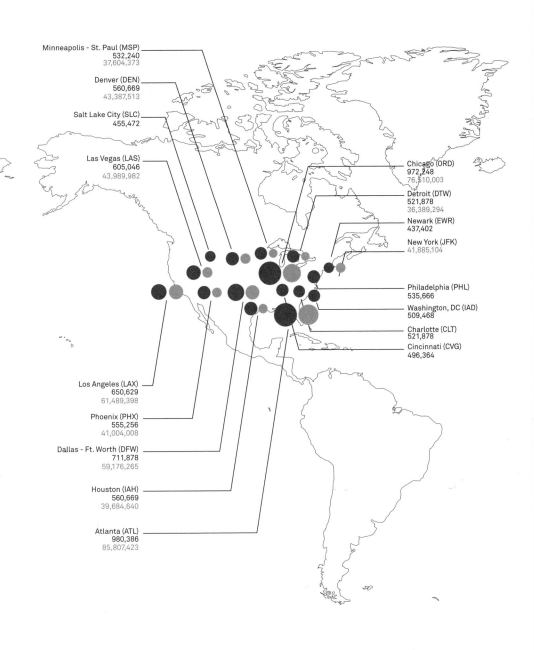

Minneapolis - St. Paul (MSP)
532,240
37,604,373

Denver (DEN)
560,669
43,387,513

Salt Lake City (SLC)
455,472

Las Vegas (LAS)
605,046
43,989,982

Chicago (ORD)
972,248
76,510,003

Detroit (DTW)
521,878
36,389,294

Newark (EWR)
437,402

New York (JFK)
41,885,104

Philadelphia (PHL)
535,666

Washington, DC (IAD)
509,468

Charlotte (CLT)
521,878

Cincinnati (CVG)
496,364

Los Angeles (LAX)
650,629
61,489,398

Phoenix (PHX)
555,256
41,004,008

Dallas - Ft. Worth (DFW)
711,878
59,176,265

Houston (IAH)
560,669
39,684,640

Atlanta (ATL)
980,386
85,807,423

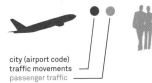

city (airport code)
traffic movements
passenger traffic

Traffic Movement: total number of landings plus takeoffs of aircraft
Passenger Traffic: total passengers enplaned and deplaned

Periodic target for Shanghai Aviation Hub Development

Phase two period one project
2005-2007, preparatory and initial period: to lay a good foundation for hub construction. Specific tasks include: basically complete the construction of the Phase Two Project of Pudong international Airport. The passengers throughout of the two airports will reach 49 million person-time, cargo and mail throughout will reach 2.5 million tons, and essentially establish the position of an international air cargo hub.

Phase two period two project
2007-2010, adjusting and upgrading period: basically complete the building of Shanghai Aviation Hub. Specific tasks include: All the Phase Two Project facilities will be put into operation. The renovation and expansion projects of Hongqiao International Airport will be fundamentally completed. The passenger throughput and cargo throughput of the two airports will reach 80 million person-time and 4.1 million tons respectively, thus becoming the largest cargo transport hub in Asia.

Long range period project
2010-2015, ripe and expanding period: to ensure the position of Shanghai aviation hub in an all around. Specific tasks include: the passenger and cargo throughputs rank respectively the top level in the Asia-Pacific region, attaining 100 million person-time and 7 million tons respectively. Four runways will be available in Pudong International Airport. The air traffic control capacity will reach the world advanced level, the hub airline network with Shanghai as the center will ripen , and numbers of available air routes and weekly flight frequencies will surpass the average level of world hub airports.

Source: Shanghai Urban Planning Exhibition Center

Shanghai Freight Traffic Volume

1980–2005

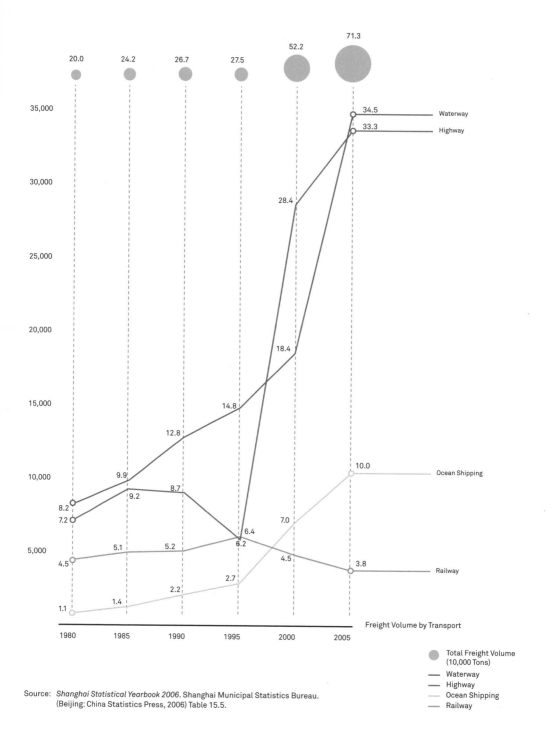

20.0	24.2	26.7	27.5	52.2	71.3

35,000 — Waterway 34.5

— Highway 33.3

30,000

28.4

25,000

20,000

18.4

15,000 — 14.8

12.8

10,000 — 9.9 — 8.7 — Ocean Shipping 10.0

9.2

8.2

7.2 — 7.0

6.4

6.2 — Railway 3.8

5,000 — 5.1 — 5.2 — 4.5

4.5 — 2.7

2.2

1.4

1.1

Freight Volume by Transport

1980   1985   1990   1995   2000   2005

● Total Freight Volume (10,000 Tons)
— Waterway
— Highway
— Ocean Shipping
— Railway

Source: *Shanghai Statistical Yearbook 2006*. Shanghai Municipal Statistics Bureau. (Beijing: China Statistics Press, 2006) Table 15.5.

China Freight Traffic Volume

1980-2005

144,701	133,662	126,903	119,287	111,233
Shandong	Shanxi	Zhejiang	Guangdong	Jiangsu
7.7%	7.1%	6.8%	6.4%	5.9%

95,558	88,342	78,699	77,534	69,187
Lionging	Hebei	Henan	Hunan	Inner Mongolia
5.1%	4.7%	4.2%	4.1%	3.7%

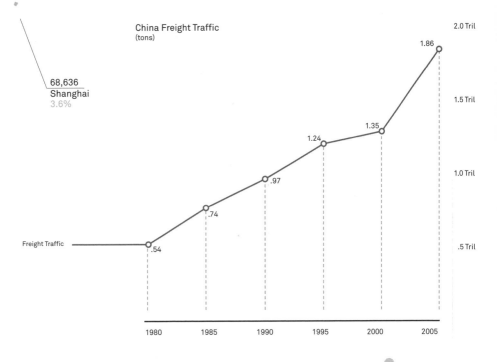

68,636
Shanghai
3.6%

China Freight Traffic
(tons)

2.0 Tril

1.86

1.5 Tril

1.35

1.24

1.0 Tril

.97

.74

Freight Traffic

.54

.5 Tril

1980   1985   1990   1995   2000   2005

Freight Traffic
(10,000 tons)
administrative area
% of China Total

Source: *China Statistical Yearbook 2006*. National Bureau of Statistics of China.
(Beijing: China Statistics Press, 2006) Table 16.14, 16.8.

Ports
1980-2005

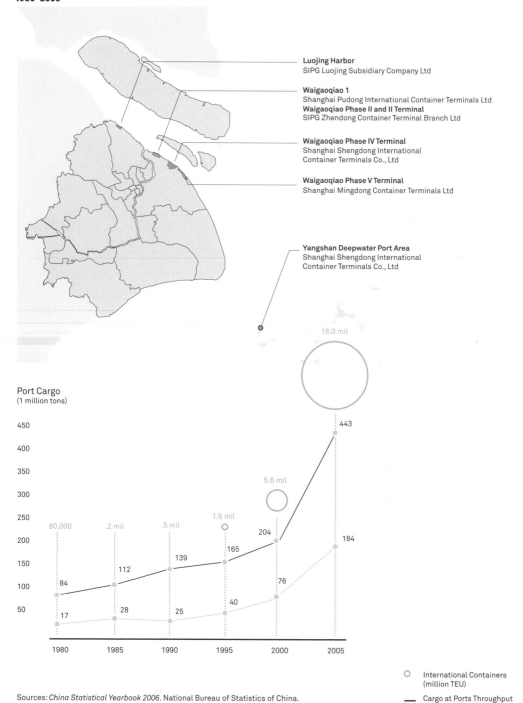

Luojing Harbor
SIPG Luojing Subsidiary Company Ltd

Waigaoqiao 1
Shanghai Pudong International Container Terminals Ltd
Waigaoqiao Phase II and II Terminal
SIPG Zhendong Container Terminal Branch Ltd

Waigaoqiao Phase IV Terminal
Shanghai Shengdong International
Container Terminals Co., Ltd

Waigaoqiao Phase V Terminal
Shanghai Mingdong Container Terminals Ltd

Yangshan Deepwater Port Area
Shanghai Shengdong International
Container Terminals Co., Ltd

18.0 mil

Port Cargo
(1 million tons)

5.6 mil

450   443

400

350

300

250   1.5 mil

80,000   .2 mil   .5 mil   204
200   184

150   112   139   165

100   84   76

50   17   28   25   40

1980   1985   1990   1995   2000   2005

○   International Containers
    (million TEU)

▬   Cargo at Ports Throughput

▬   Cargo Throughput of
    Foreign Trade

Sources: *China Statistical Yearbook 2006*. National Bureau of Statistics of China.
(Beijing: China Statistics Press, 2006) Table 15.7, 15.8

Length and Area of Shanghai Terminals

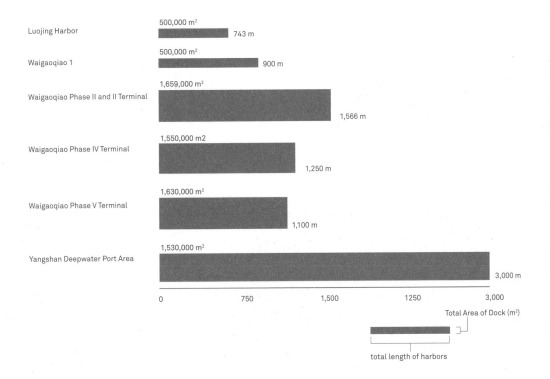

Luojing Harbor

500,000 m²

743 m

Waigaoqiao 1

500,000 m²

900 m

Waigaoqiao Phase II and II Terminal

1,659,000 m²

1,566 m

Waigaoqiao Phase IV Terminal

1,550,000 m2

1,250 m

Waigaoqiao Phase V Terminal

1,630,000 m²

1,100 m

Yangshan Deepwater Port Area

1,530,000 m²

3,000 m

| 0 | 750 | 1,500 | 1,250 | 3,000 |

Total Area of Dock (m²)

total length of harbors

Length and Number of Berths
for Combined Terminals of Shanghai

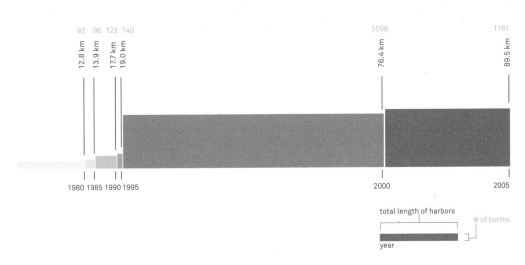

92   98   122   140

12.8 km   13.9 km   17.7 km   19.0 km

1098

76.4 km

1181

89.5 km

1980 1985 1990 1995

2000

2005

total length of harbors

# of berths

year

Shanghai International Shipping Center Yangshan Deepwater Port Area

Master Plan
Located near the estuary of Hangzhou Bay away from the mouth of the Yangtze River, 27.5 km (sea surface linear distance) southeast of Luchaogang in Nanhui District of Shanghai and 104 km. away from the international shipping line, Yangshan Port is a superior deepwater port of Shanghai International Shipping Center with water depth of over 15 meters closest to Shanghai.
According to the master plan, the port along the Da Yangshan and Xiao Yangshan island chain is divided into the two parts of south terminal and north terminal with a single water passageway.

Under the master plan, Xiao Yangshan, or the northern part of the port, is planned to have a deepwater coastline of more than 10 km. for over 30 berths with an annual capacity of more than 14.4 million TEUs before 2012. The 10 km. of deepwater coastline along Da Yangshan, or the southern part of the port, will be reserved for the future development of the port area.

Yangshan Port Area
The first phase of the project saw the development of 5 large container berths between Xiao Yangshan and Huogaitang with docks totaling 1,600 m. in length.

These docks can accommodate container vessels of the fifth and sixth generations as well as those with a capacity of 8,000 TEU. Stacking yards, warehouses, roads, auxiliary facilities and handling equipment were put in place in the port, which covers a total land area of 1.17 km^2 and 9 km. of access channel were also dredged. It was completed in 2005.
The second phase of the project completed the construction of 4 berthing spaces, which started pilot running on December 10, 2006.

Source: Shanghai Urban Planning Exhibition Center

Donghai Bridge

Donghai Bridge starts from the northernmost point at the intersection between the current dam and the beach which is 4 km. to the east and 1.4 km. to the north of Lunchaogang passenger terminal in Nanhui District, spans Hangzhou Bay, extends to the southernmost point and ends in the port area at Xiaochengzi Hill of Qiqu archipielago in Shengsi County, Zhejiang Province.
The bridge is 31.5 km. long and 31.5 m. wide with two-way six lanes and a designed vehicle speed of 80 km/h.
There is one main opening (net height is 40 m. and the clear width is 400 meters, and every bridge pier is designed to have a capacity to resist 10,000 DWT ship collision) allowing passage of 5,000 ton-class vessels, one secondary opening allowing passage of 1,000 ton-class ships and two openings for 500 ton-class ships.
Pipes and cables for water and electricity supply as well as communication are also connected to the port area via the bridge.
Donghai Bridge, with designed life of 100 years, became the major passage way for land container transportation and distribution, when completed at the same time as the port and opened to traffic at the end of 2005.

Source: Shanghai Urban Planning Exhibition Center

Commercial and Industrial Uses
2020

Yangtze River

Huangpu River

Hangzhou Bay

Commercial & Public Facilities
Warehouse
Industrial

N

0 1   5   10   20 km

Source: *Summary of the Comprehensive Plan of Shanghai (1999-2020)*. Shanghai Urban Planning Administration Bureau. Shanghai Urban Planning and Design Research Institute.

Industrial Value
2005

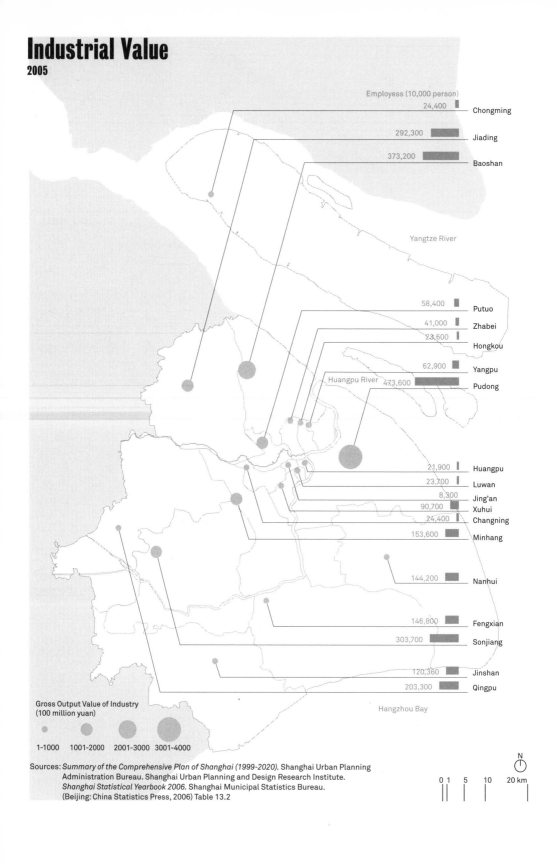

Employess (10,000 person)

24,400 — Chongming

292,300 — Jiading

373,200 — Baoshan

Yangtze River

58,400 — Putuo

41,000 — Zhabei

23,600 — Hongkou

62,900 — Yangpu

Huangpu River 473,600 — Pudong

21,900 — Huangpu

23,700 — Luwan

8,300 — Jing'an

90,700 — Xuhui

24,400 — Changning

153,600 — Minhang

144,200 — Nanhui

146,800 — Fengxian

303,700 — Sonjiang

120,360 — Jinshan

203,300 — Qingpu

Hangzhou Bay

Gross Output Value of Industry
(100 million yuan)

1-1000   1001-2000   2001-3000   3001-4000

Sources: *Summary of the Comprehensive Plan of Shanghai (1999-2020).* Shanghai Urban Planning
Administration Bureau. Shanghai Urban Planning and Design Research Institute.
Shanghai Statistical Yearbook 2006. Shanghai Municipal Statistics Bureau.
(Beijing: China Statistics Press, 2006) Table 13.2

N

0 1   5   10   20 km

Value Added of
Key Manufacturing Industries
(100 million yuan)

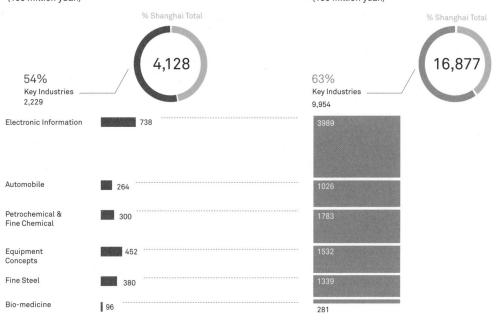

% Shanghai Total

4,128

54%
Key Industries
2,229

Electronic Information — 738

Automobile — 264

Petrochemical &
Fine Chemical — 300

Equipment
Concepts — 452

Fine Steel — 380

Bio-medicine — 96

Gross Output Value of
Key Manufacturing Industries
(100 million yuan)

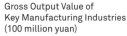

% Shanghai Total

16,877

63%
Key Industries
9,954

3989

1026

1783

1532

1339

281

Value Added of Six Pillar Industries
(100 million yuan)

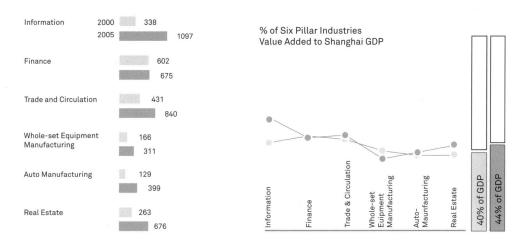

Information	2000	338
	2005	1097
Finance		602
		675
Trade and Circulation		431
		840
Whole-set Equipment Manufacturing		166
		311
Auto Manufacturing		129
		399
Real Estate		263
		676

% of Six Pillar Industries
Value Added to Shanghai GDP

Information
Finance
Trade & Circulation
Whole-set Equipment Manufacturing
Auto-Maunfacturing
Real Estate

40% of GDP
44% of GDP

Source: *Shanghai Statistical Yearbook 2006*. Shanghai Municipal Statistics Bureau.
(Beijing: China Statistics Press, 2006) Table 13.7.

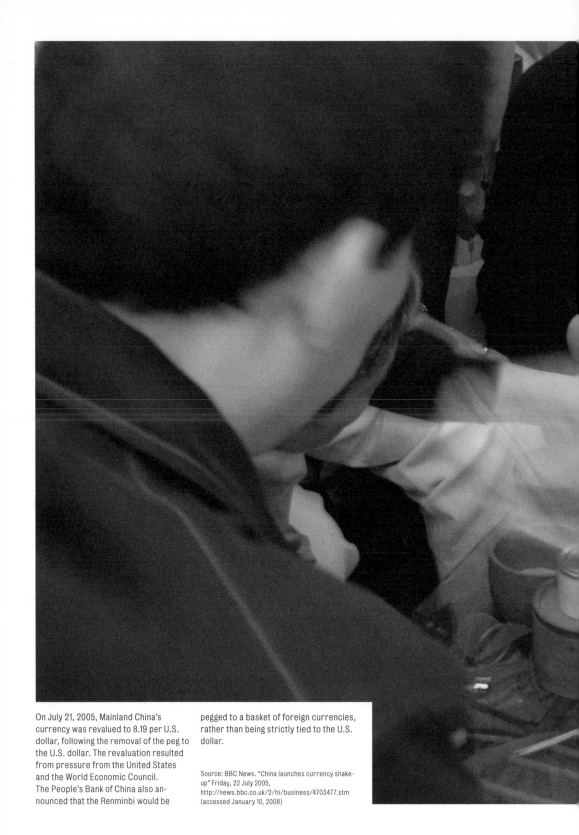

On July 21, 2005, Mainland China's currency was revalued to 8.19 per U.S. dollar, following the removal of the peg to the U.S. dollar. The revaluation resulted from pressure from the United States and the World Economic Council. The People's Bank of China also announced that the Renminbi would be pegged to a basket of foreign currencies, rather than being strictly tied to the U.S. dollar.

Source: BBC News. "China launches currency shake-up" Friday, 22 July 2005, http://news.bbc.co.uk/2/hi/business/4703477.stm (accessed January 10, 2008)

Imports and Exports

1980–2005

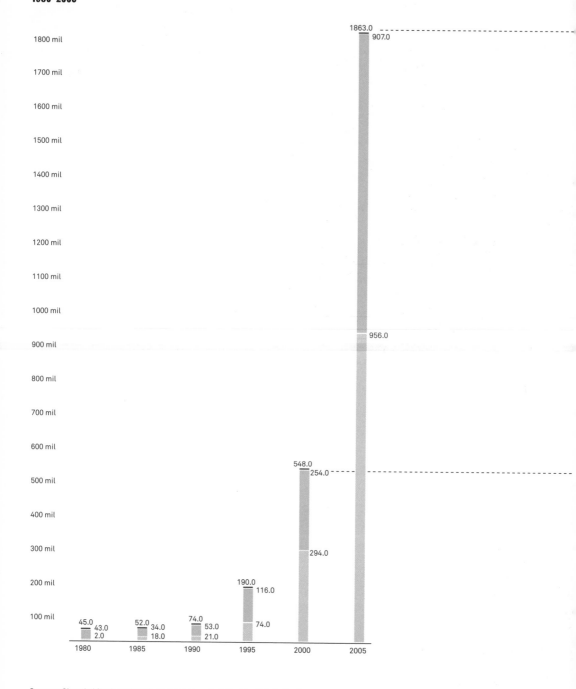

1800 mil

1700 mil

1600 mil

1500 mil

1400 mil

1300 mil

1200 mil

1100 mil

1000 mil

900 mil

800 mil

700 mil

600 mil

500 mil

400 mil

300 mil

200 mil

100 mil

1863.0
907.0

956.0

548.0
254.0

294.0

190.0
116.0

74.0

45.0
43.0
2.0

52.0
34.0
18.0

74.0
53.0
21.0

1980   1985   1990   1995   2000   2005

Sources: *Shanghai Statistical Yearbook 2006*. Shanghai Municipal Statistics Bureau.
(Beijing: China Statistics Press, 2006) Table 8.1, 8.2, 8.3, 8.4.
China Statistical Yearbook 2006. National Bureau of Statistics of China.
(Beijing: China Statistics Press, 2006) Table 18.3.

- - - - - - - - - - - - - - 2005 Exports

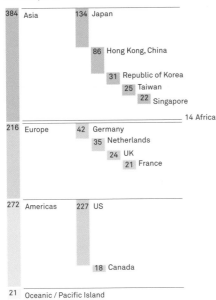

384 Asia   134 Japan

86 Hong Kong, China

31 Republic of Korea
25 Taiwan
22 Singapore

14 Africa

216 Europe   42 Germany
35 Netherlands
24 UK
21 France

272 Americas   227 US

18 Canada

21 Oceanic / Pacific Island

2005 Imports

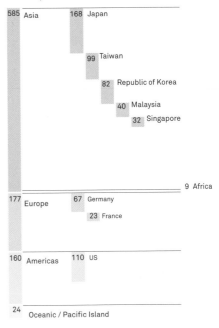

585 Asia   168 Japan

99 Taiwan

82 Republic of Korea

40 Malaysia
32 Singapore

9 Africa

177 Europe   67 Germany

23 France

160 Americas   110 US

24 Oceanic / Pacific Island

China Ports Exports 2005

Other Ports
5,496,000,000

7620

24.7% Shanghai
2,124,000,000

China Ports Imports 2005

Other Ports
5,219,000,000

6601

21.0% Shanghai
1,382,000,000

- - - - - - - - - - - - - 2000 Exports

129 Asia   60 Japan

6 Africa

46 Europe
68 Americas   56 US

5

Oceanic / Pacific Island

2000 Imports

161 Asia   70 Japan
20 Republic of Korea

2 Africa

63 Europe   26 Germany
59 Americas   40 US

8

Oceanic / Pacific Island

Total

Exports
(100 million USD)

Imports
(100 million USD)

Employment Sectors
2000–2005

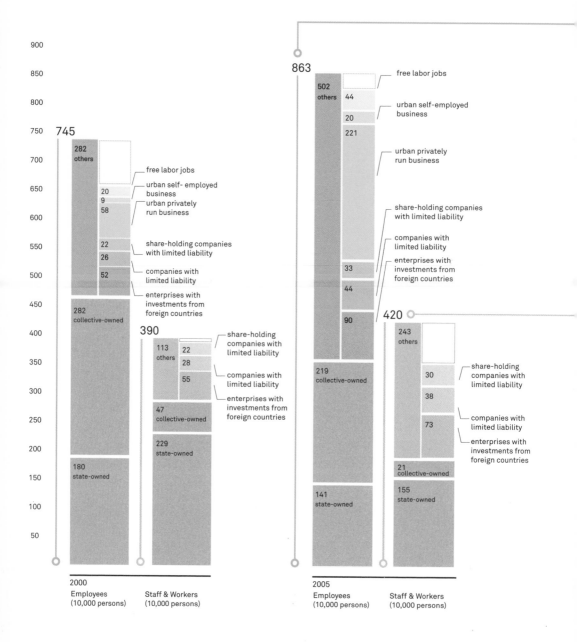

745

282
others

free labor jobs

20
urban self- employed
business
9
58
urban privately
run business

22
share-holding companies
with limited liability
26

52
companies with
limited liability

enterprises with
investments from
foreign countries

282
collective-owned

390

113
others
22
share-holding
companies with
limited liability
28

55
companies with
limited liability

enterprises with
investments from
foreign countries

47
collective-owned

180
state-owned

229
state-owned

2000
Employees
(10,000 persons)

Staff & Workers
(10,000 persons)

863

502
others
44
free labor jobs

20
urban self-employed
business
221

urban privately
run business

share-holding companies
with limited liability

companies with
limited liability

33
enterprises with
investments from
foreign countries

44

90

219
collective-owned

420

243
others

share-holding
companies with
limited liability
30

38

companies with
limited liability
73

enterprises with
investments from
foreign countries

141
state-owned

21
collective-owned

155
state-owned

2005
Employees
(10,000 persons)

Staff & Workers
(10,000 persons)

900
850
800
750
700
650
600
550
500
450
400
350
300
250
200
150
100
50

Source: *Shanghai Statistical Yearbook 2006*. Shanghai Municipal Statistics Bureau.
(Beijing: China Statistics Press, 2006) Table 3.13.

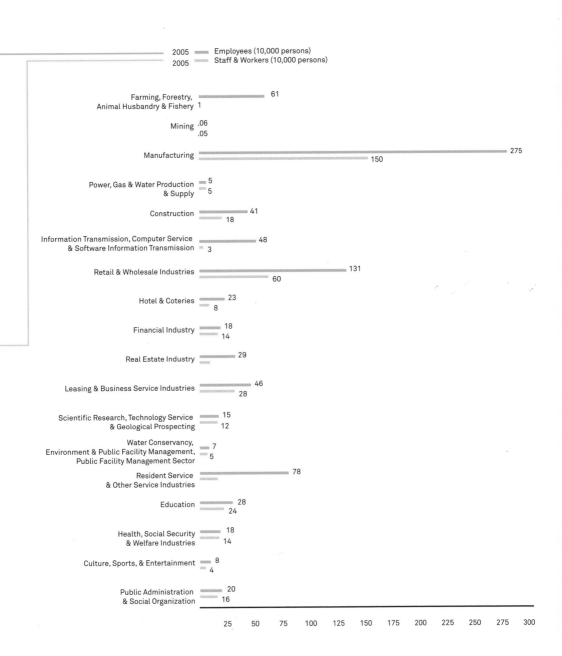

2005 — Employees (10,000 persons)
2005 — Staff & Workers (10,000 persons)

Farming, Forestry, Animal Husbandry & Fishery: 61 / 1

Mining: .06 / .05

Manufacturing: 275 / 150

Power, Gas & Water Production & Supply: 5 / 5

Construction: 41 / 18

Information Transmission, Computer Service & Software Information Transmission: 48 / 3

Retail & Wholesale Industries: 131 / 60

Hotel & Coteries: 23 / 8

Financial Industry: 18 / 14

Real Estate Industry: 29

Leasing & Business Service Industries: 46 / 28

Scientific Research, Technology Service & Geological Prospecting: 15 / 12

Water Conservancy, Environment & Public Facility Management, Public Facility Management Sector: 7 / 5

Resident Service & Other Service Industries: 78

Education: 28 / 24

Health, Social Security & Welfare Industries: 18 / 14

Culture, Sports, & Entertainment: 8 / 4

Public Administration & Social Organization: 20 / 16

25   50   75   100   125   150   175   200   225   250   275   300

Source: *Shanghai Statistical Yearbook 2006*. Shanghai Municipal Statistics Bureau. (Beijing: China Statistics Press, 2006) Table 3.14, 3.15.

Foreign Residents and Workers
2005

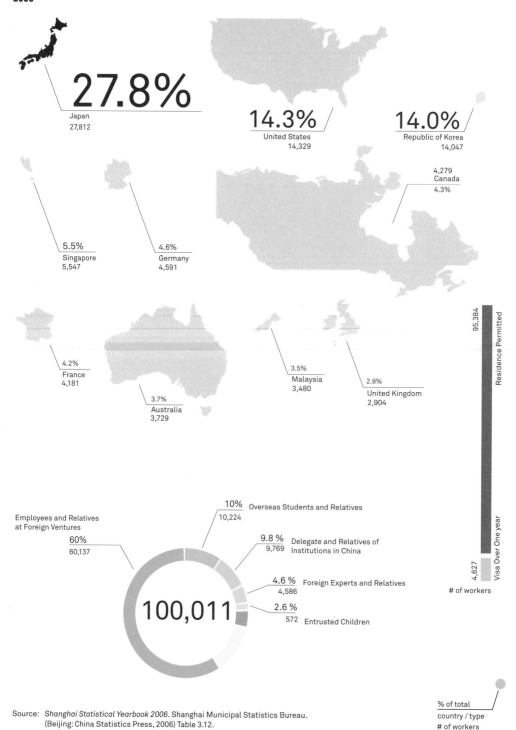

27.8%
Japan
27,812

14.3%
United States
14,329

14.0%
Republic of Korea
14,047

4,279
Canada
4.3%

5.5%
Singapore
5,547

4.6%
Germany
4,591

4.2%
France
4,181

3.7%
Australia
3,729

3.5%
Malaysia
3,480

2.9%
United Kingdom
2,904

95,384 — Residence Permitted

4,627 — Visa Over One year

# of workers

10% Overseas Students and Relatives
10,224

9.8 % Delegate and Relatives of
9,769 Institutions in China

Employees and Relatives
at Foreign Ventures
60%
60,137

4.6 % Foreign Experts and Relatives
4,586

2.6 %
572 Entrusted Children

100,011

% of total
country / type
# of workers

Source: *Shanghai Statistical Yearbook 2006*. Shanghai Municipal Statistics Bureau.
(Beijing: China Statistics Press, 2006) Table 3.12.

New Urban Employment
1980-2005

World Largest Country Labor Force

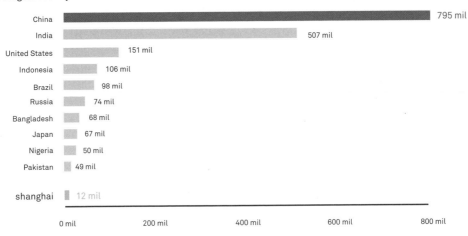

China	795 mil
India	507 mil
United States	151 mil
Indonesia	106 mil
Brazil	98 mil
Russia	74 mil
Bangladesh	68 mil
Japan	67 mil
Nigeria	50 mil
Pakistan	49 mil
shanghai	12 mil

0 mil   200 mil   400 mil   600 mil   800 mil

New Urban Employment & Retirement

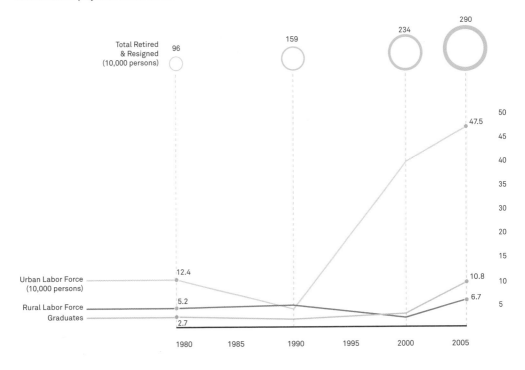

Total Retired & Resigned (10,000 persons)   96   159   234   290

Urban Labor Force (10,000 persons)   12.4   10.8

Rural Labor Force   5.2   6.7

Graduates   2.7

47.5

1980   1985   1990   1995   2000   2005

Sources: *Shanghai Statistical Yearbook 2006*. Shanghai Municipal Statistics Bureau.
(Beijing: China Statistics Press, 2006) Table 3.12, 3.24
United States. Central Intelligence Agency. "The World Factbook 2006." CIA World Factbook,
https://www.cia.gov/library/publications/the-world-factbook/index.html. (accessed May, 15, 2007).

District Expenditure
2000–2005

Districts and Counties Fiscal Expenditure versus Fiscal Revenue

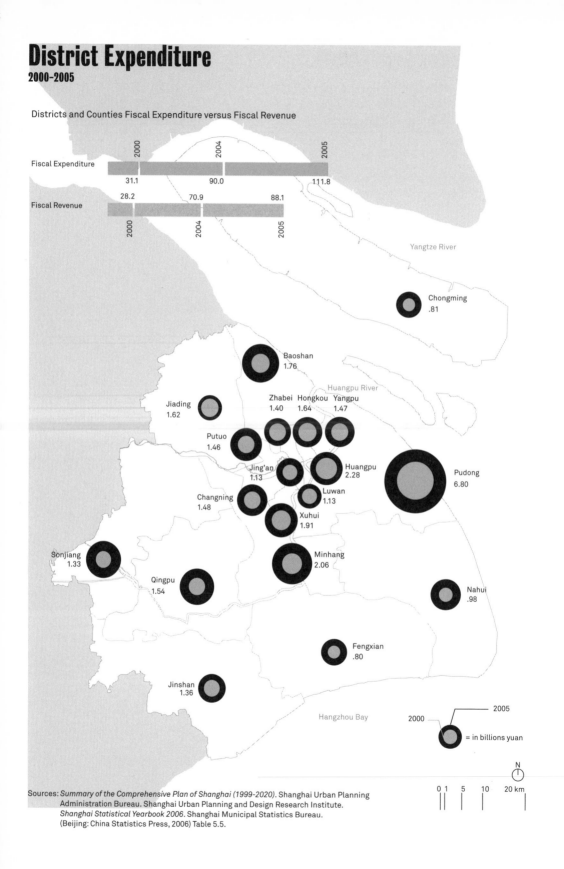

Fiscal Expenditure

2000   2004   2005

31.1   90.0   111.8

Fiscal Revenue

28.2   70.9   88.1

2000   2004   2005

Yangtze River

Chongming
.81

Baoshan
1.76

Huangpu River

Jiading
1.62

Zhabei
1.40

Hongkou
1.64

Yangpu
1.47

Putuo
1.46

Jing'an
1.13

Huangpu
2.28

Pudong
6.80

Luwan
1.13

Changning
1.48

Xuhui
1.91

Sonjiang
1.33

Minhang
2.06

Nahui
.98

Qingpu
1.54

Fengxian
.80

Jinshan
1.36

Hangzhou Bay

2005

2000

= in billions yuan

N

0 1   5   10   20 km

Sources: *Summary of the Comprehensive Plan of Shanghai (1999-2020)*. Shanghai Urban Planning
Administration Bureau. Shanghai Urban Planning and Design Research Institute.
Shanghai Statistical Yearbook 2006. Shanghai Municipal Statistics Bureau.
(Beijing: China Statistics Press, 2006) Table 5.5.

Government Expenditure

2005

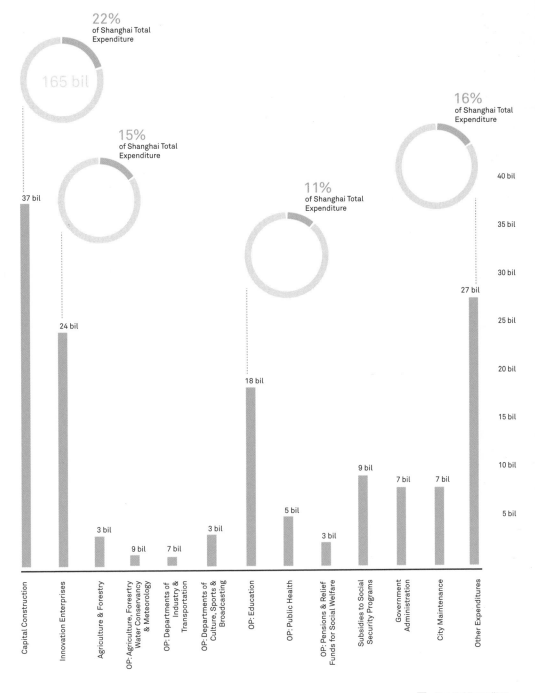

22%
of Shanghai Total
Expenditure

165 bil

16%
of Shanghai Total
Expenditure

40 bil

15%
of Shanghai Total
Expenditure

37 bil

11%
of Shanghai Total
Expenditure

35 bil

30 bil

24 bil

27 bil

25 bil

20 bil

18 bil

15 bil

10 bil

9 bil   7 bil   7 bil

3 bil   3 bil   5 bil
         9 bil 7 bil   3 bil

5 bil

Capital Construction

Innovation Enterprises

Agriculture & Forestry

OP: Agriculture, Forestry Water Conservancy & Meteorology

OP: Departments of Industry & Transportation

OP: Departments of Culture, Sports & Broadcasting

OP: Education

OP: Public Health

OP: Pensions & Relief Funds for Social Welfare

Subsidies to Social Security Programs

Government Administration

City Maintenance

Other Expenditures

Shanghai Expenditure
(billion yuan)
OP: Operating Expense

Source: *China Statistical Yearbook 2006*. National Bureau of Statistics of China.
(Beijing: China Statistics Press, 2006) Table 8.15.

Tourism

1978-2005

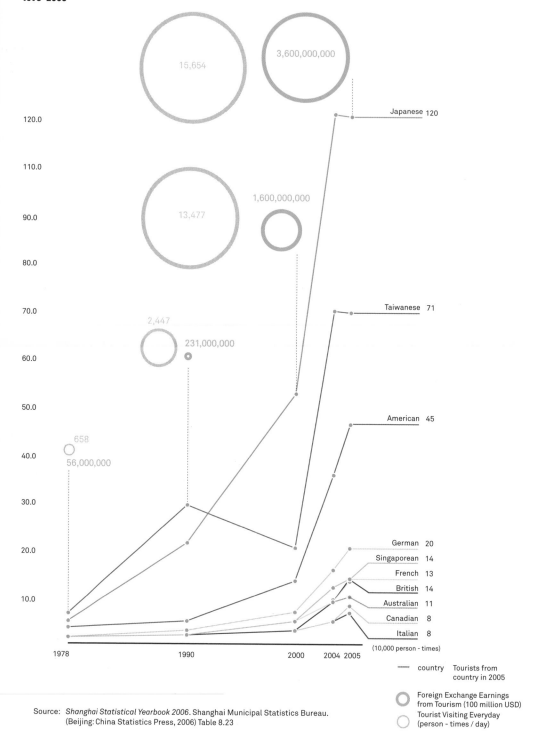

15,654

3,600,000,000

120.0 — Japanese 120

110.0

13,477

1,600,000,000

90.0

80.0

2,447

70.0 — Taiwanese 71

231,000,000

60.0

American 45

50.0

658

40.0

56,000,000

30.0

20.0 — German 20
Singaporean 14
French 13
British 14
Australian 11
Canadian 8
10.0 — Italian 8

1978   1990   2000   2004 2005
(10,000 person - times)

—— country   Tourists from
              country in 2005

◎ Foreign Exchange Earnings
  from Tourism (100 million USD)
○ Tourist Visiting Everyday
  (person - times / day)

Source: *Shanghai Statistical Yearbook 2006*. Shanghai Municipal Statistics Bureau.
(Beijing: China Statistics Press, 2006) Table 8.23

Shanghai Total Gross Domestic Product

1980–2005

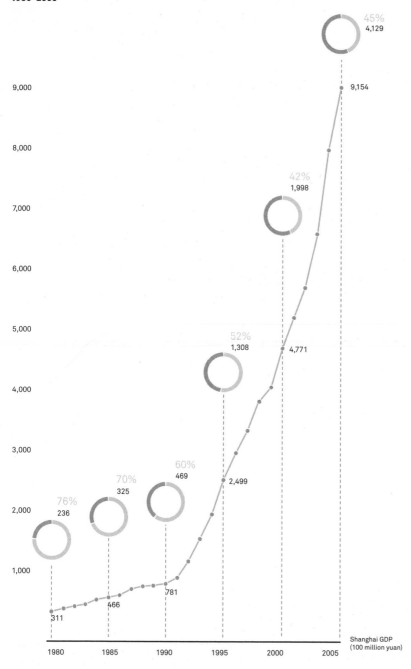

45%
4,129

9,000 — 9,154

8,000 —

7,000 —

42%
1,998

6,000 —

5,000 —

52%
1,308

4,771

4,000 —

3,000 —

60%
469

70%
325

2,499

2,000 —

76%
236

1,000 —

781

466

311

| 1980 | 1985 | 1990 | 1995 | 2000 | 2005 |

Shanghai GDP
(100 million yuan)

% of Secondary Industry
Value in Total GDP

Value of Secondary
Industry Total GDP

Source: *Shanghai Statistical Yearbook 2006*. Shanghai Municipal Statistics Bureau.
(Beijing: China Statistics Press, 2006) Table 4.1.

Shanghai Gross Domestic Product per Capita
1980-2005

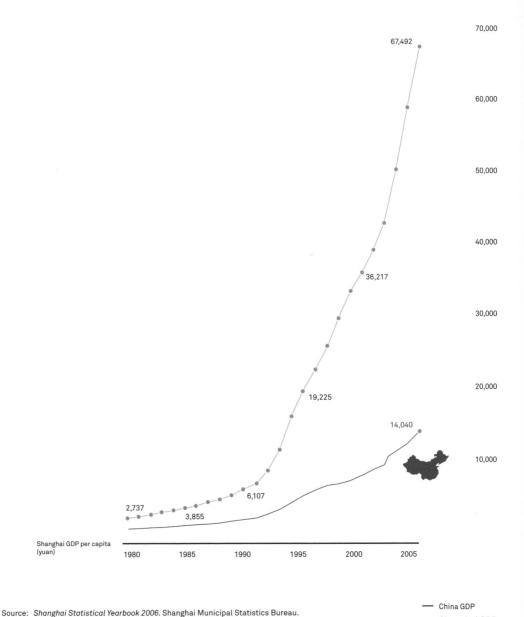

Shanghai GDP per capita (yuan)

67,492

36,217

19,225

14,040

6,107

2,737

3,855

70,000

60,000

50,000

40,000

30,000

20,000

10,000

1980   1985   1990   1995   2000   2005

Source: *Shanghai Statistical Yearbook 2006.* Shanghai Municipal Statistics Bureau.
(Beijing: China Statistics Press, 2006) Table 4.1.

——— China GDP
——— Shanghai GDP

China's Total Gross Domestic Product

1980–2005

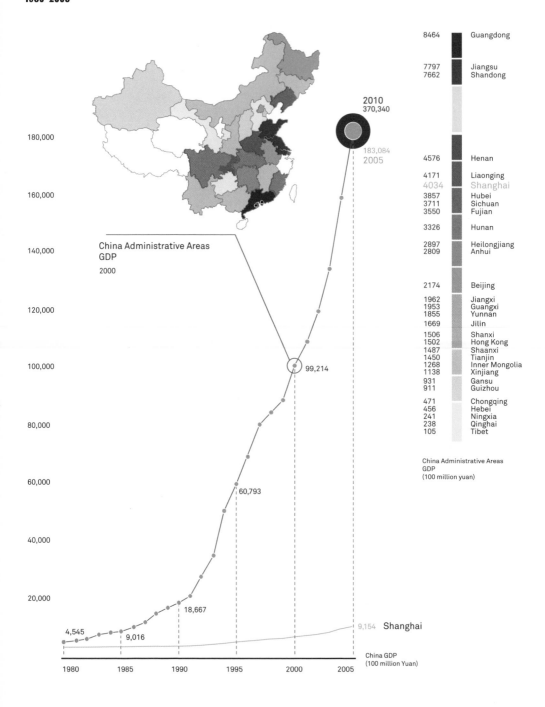

8464	Guangdong
7797	Jiangsu
7662	Shandong
4576	Henan
4171	Liaonging
4034	Shanghai
3857	Hubei
3711	Sichuan
3550	Fujian
3326	Hunan
2897	Heilongjiang
2809	Anhui
2174	Beijing
1962	Jiangxi
1953	Guangxi
1855	Yunnan
1669	Jilin
1506	Shanxi
1502	Hong Kong
1487	Shaanxi
1450	Tianjin
1268	Inner Mongolia
1138	Xinjiang
931	Gansu
911	Guizhou
471	Chongqing
456	Hebei
241	Ningxia
238	Qinghai
105	Tibet

China Administrative Areas
GDP
(100 million yuan)

2010
370,340

183,084
2005

China Administrative Areas
GDP
2000

99,214

60,793

18,667

4,545

9,016

9,154 Shanghai

China GDP
(100 million Yuan)

China GDP
Shanghai GDP

Sources: *China Statistical Yearbook 2006*. National Bureau of Statistics of China.
(Beijing: China Statistics Press, 2006) Table 3.1
International Monetary Fund, World Economic Outlook Database April 2008,
http://www.imf.org/external/pubs/ft/weo/2008/01/weodata/index.aspx
(accessed April20, 2008).

China's Gross Domestic Product per Capita

1980–2005

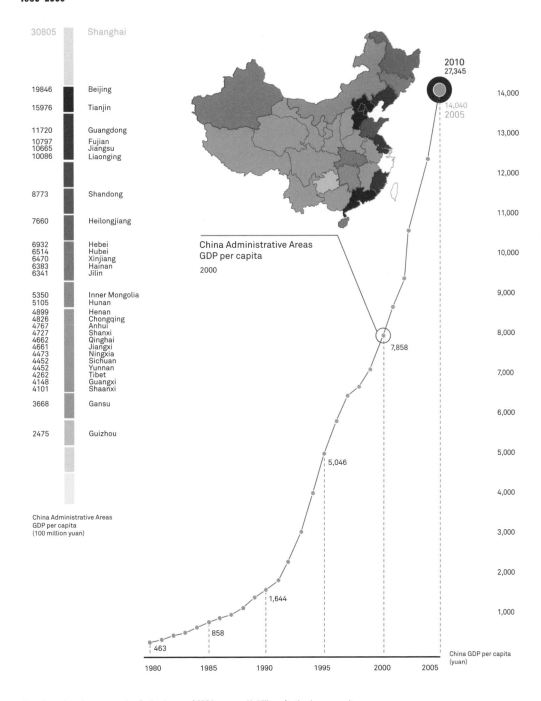

Value	Region
30805	Shanghai
19846	Beijing
15976	Tianjin
11720	Guangdong
10797	Fujian
10665	Jiangsu
10086	Liaonging
8773	Shandong
7660	Heilongjiang
6932	Hebei
6514	Hubei
6470	Xinjiang
6383	Hainan
6341	Jilin
5350	Inner Mongolia
5105	Hunan
4899	Henan
4826	Chongqing
4767	Anhui
4727	Shanxi
4662	Qinghai
4661	Jiangxi
4473	Ningxia
4452	Sichuan
4452	Yunnan
4262	Tibet
4148	Guangxi
4101	Shaanxi
3668	Gansu
2475	Guizhou

China Administrative Areas
GDP per capita
(100 million yuan)

China Administrative Areas
GDP per capita
2000

2010
27,345

14,040
2005

14,000

13,000

12,000

11,000

10,000

9,000

8,000

7,858

7,000

6,000

5,046

5,000

4,000

3,000

2,000

1,644

1,000

858

463

China GDP per capita
(yuan)

1980   1985   1990   1995   2000   2005

Gross domestic product, current prices (national currency) GDP is expressed in billions of national currency units.

Gross domestic product per capita, current prices (national currency) GDP is expressed in current national currency per person. Data are derived by dividing current price GDP by total population.

[1] Macau calculation based on MOP conversion to yuan

[2] Hong Kong calculation based on HKD conversion to MOP to yuan

World's Largest Gross Domestic Products

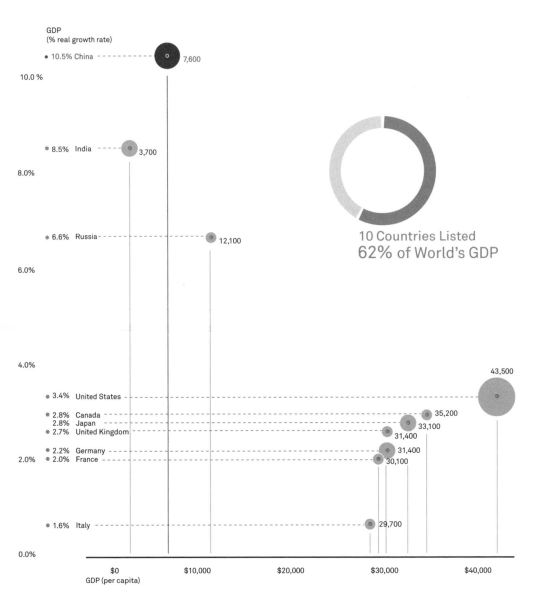

GDP
(% real growth rate)

- 10.5% China ---- 7,600
10.0 %
- 8.5% India --- 3,700
8.0%
- 6.6% Russia --- 12,100
6.0%
4.0%
43,500
- 3.4% United States ---
- 2.8% Canada --- 35,200
- 2.8% Japan --- 33,100
- 2.7% United Kingdom --- 31,400
- 2.2% Germany --- 31,400
2.0% - 2.0% France --- 30,100
- 1.6% Italy --- 29,700
0.0%

$0 $10,000 $20,000 $30,000 $40,000
GDP (per capita)

10 Countries Listed
62% of World's GDP

Sources: International Monetary Fund, World Economic Outlook Database April 2008
http://www.imf.org/external/pubs/ft/weo/2008/01/weodata/index.aspx
accessed April20, 2008).
United States. Central Intelligence Agency. The World Factbook 2006.
https://www.cia.gov/library/publications/the-world-factbook/index.html

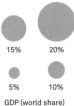

15%   20%

5%   10%

GDP (world share)

132

World Cities: Gross Domestic Product per Capita

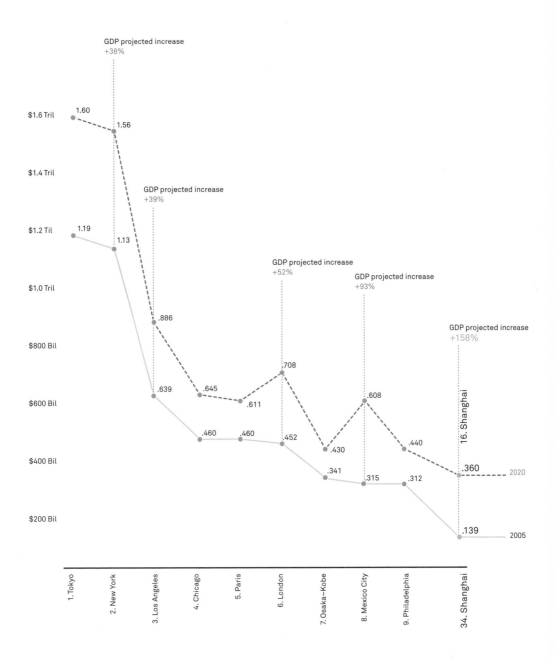

GDP projected increase
+38%

GDP projected increase
+39%

GDP projected increase
+52%

GDP projected increase
+93%

GDP projected increase
+158%

$1.6 Tril 1.60
1.56

$1.4 Tril

$1.2 Til 1.19
1.13

$1.0 Tril

.886

$800 Bil

.708

$600 Bil .639 .645
.611

.460 .460 .452 .608

$400 Bil .430 .440
.341 .360   2020
.315 .312

16. Shanghai

$200 Bil .139   2005

1. Tokyo
2. New York
3. Los Angeles
4. Chicago
5. Paris
6. London
7. Osaka–Kobe
8. Mexico City
9. Philadelphia
34. Shanghai

Sources: City Mayors, "Richest Cities and Urban Areas in 2005," "Richest Cities and Urban Areas in 2020,"
   Ed. Tann vom Hove. City Mayors.
   http://www.citymayors.com/statistics/richest-cities-2020.html
   http://www.citymayors.com/statistics/richest-cities-2005.html
   (accessed July 30, 2007).

Total GDP
(Purchase Power Parity
   in billions USD)
- - - 2020 Projected Total GDP
—— 2005 Total GDP

Parent Transnational Corporations and Foreign Affiliates

Selected Years

United Kingdom
2,360
13,667

Korea†
400
13,311

Germany
5.855
9,193

5x

China
3,429
280,000

Phillipines *
na
311

Japan
4,563
4,500

Australia †
1,380
1,991

Source: Based on *UNCTAD World Investment Report* (1998, 4, 4; 2004, 273, 274; 2007, 217-8).
Diagram developed from information taken from *Disaggregating the Global Economy: Shanghai*
by Saskia Sassen in this collection.

Canada **
1,439
1,439

United States *
2,418
24,607

Brazil †
165
3,549

† Refers to data collected in 2006
‡ Refers to data collected in 2002
* Refers to data collected in 2004
** Refers to data collected in 1999

numerical value to small for symbol ○

country
corporations based in the country
affiliates located in countries

Stock Exchanges by Capitalization
2002–2005

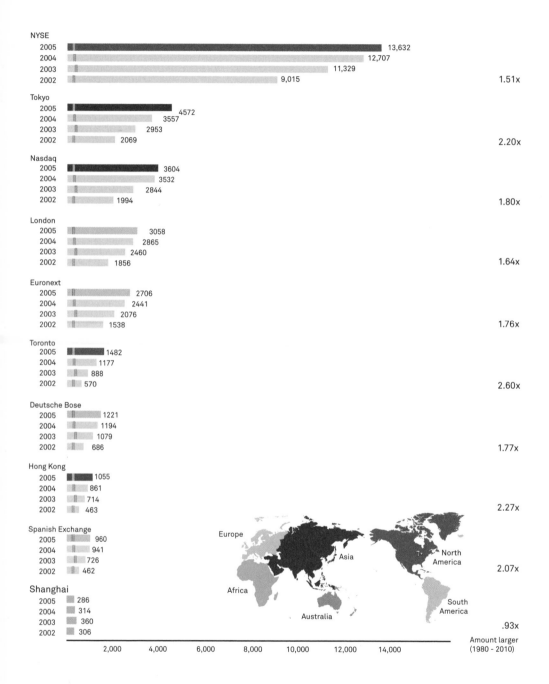

NYSE		
2005	13,632	
2004	12,707	
2003	11,329	
2002	9,015	1.51x

Tokyo		
2005	4572	
2004	3557	
2003	2953	
2002	2069	2.20x

Nasdaq		
2005	3604	
2004	3532	
2003	2844	
2002	1994	1.80x

London		
2005	3058	
2004	2865	
2003	2460	
2002	1856	1.64x

Euronext		
2005	2706	
2004	2441	
2003	2076	
2002	1538	1.76x

Toronto		
2005	1482	
2004	1177	
2003	888	
2002	570	2.60x

Deutsche Bose		
2005	1221	
2004	1194	
2003	1079	
2002	686	1.77x

Hong Kong		
2005	1055	
2004	861	
2003	714	
2002	463	2.27x

Spanish Exchange		
2005	960	
2004	941	
2003	726	
2002	462	2.07x

Shanghai		
2005	286	
2004	314	
2003	360	
2002	306	.93x

Europe
Asia
North America
Africa
South America
Australia

2,000   4,000   6,000   8,000   10,000   12,000   14,000

Amount larger
(1980 - 2010)

Source: Compiled from World Federation of Exchanges (2003, 83; 2004, 50; 2006, 118), year-end figures
with calculations of percentages added.
Diagram developed from information taken from *Disaggregating the Global Economy: Shanghai*
by Saskia Sassen in this collection.

Shanghai Stocks Publicly Issued by Enterprises

1980-2003

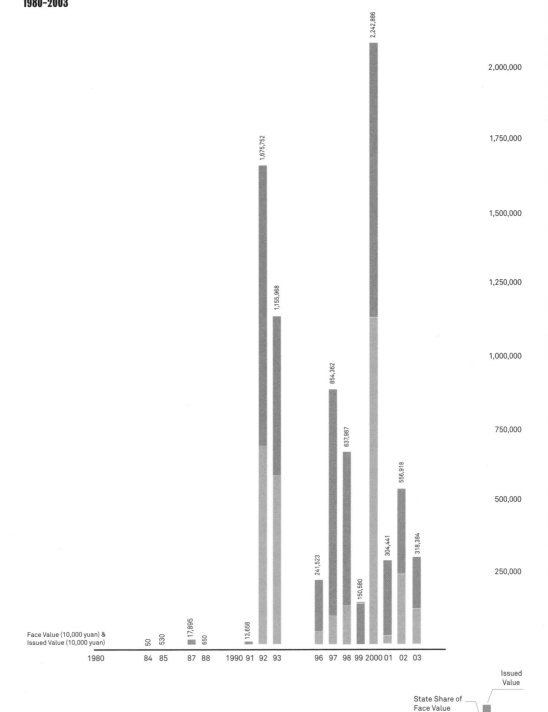

Source: *Shanghai Statistical Yearbook 2006*. Shanghai Municipal Statistics Bureau.
(Beijing: China Statistics Press, 2006) Table 17.4.

Shanghai Consumer Good Sales
1990-2005

Air Conditioners

Year	Value
2005	120,000
2000	42,000
1995	33,000
1990	1,000

Microwave Ovens

Year	Value
2005	66,000
2000	31,000
1995	23,000
1990	

Washing Machines

Year	Value
2005	65,000
2000	33,000
1995	25,000
1990	13,000

Refrigerators

Year	Value
2005	58,000
2000	33,000
1995	27,000
1990	16,000

Water Heaters

Year	Value
2005	40,000
2000	21,000
1995	28,000
1992	14,000

Range Hoods

Year	Value
2005	34,000
2000	17,000
1995	17,000
1992	8,000

Automobiles

Year	Value
2005	9,000
2000	5,000
1995	4,000
1990	

20,000 40,000 60,000 80,000 100,000 120,000 140,000

Source: *Shanghai Statistical Yearbook 2006*. Shanghai Municipal Statistics Bureau.
(Beijing: China Statistics Press, 2006) Table 16.7.

Nostalgia
Haolun Shu

Roof

The roof was a wonderland.
For me it was like the moon,
There were no skyscrapers around here.
On the roof, the world was wide open.
Adults would not cool themselves there,
The kids would go to the roof instead,
Because nobody laughed at them climbing there to cool off.
Sometimes we saw the fireworks on the roof.
Where were they fired?
In People's Square.
Could you see it from here?
Yes I could. There were no problems at all.
Now it is difficult,
Because there are so many skyscrapers around here.

Cat

Back then, the main purpose to have a cat was to catch mice.
Then, he became my pet.
In winter, when I came home from school,
I would hold the cat to warm myself, and I would play with him.
The cat is the creature of *Shikumen* alley, and they are everywhere,
They can be found in every corner
But they run fast and disappear without a trace.

Tiptoe

"Tiptoe" is the most emblematic person of Da Zhongli.
It is not because he did anything special,
He is just a cleaning man of Da Zhongli.
Since 1959, he has been waking up early in the morning and sweeping the alleys.
After, he sits by the garbage can and watches passersby until it is dark.
If he sees suspicious people, he will question them,
He will say hello to the neighbors he knows, and
The neighbors also stop to talk to him,
He almost knows all the residents of Da Zhongli and their story.
But few people in the neighborhood know his real name,
They only know his nickname, "Tiptoe."
He owes his nickname to his limp that makes him walk on tiptoe.
It was just the day I filmed him that I learned his real name, "Yuan Dehai."

Da Zhongli

One day my grandmother called me.
She told me that the newspaper said
That Da Zhongli had been sold to Hong Kong's boss by the district government.
Soon it would be demolished.
In the city of Shanghai where I live,
Neighborhood demolition and relocation is quite common.
But when I heard this, I couldn't feel common anymore,
Because it was my home.
Da Zhongli will be quite commonly demolished
To become shining skyscrapers.
Now the best I can do is to take my camera to Da Zhongli,
Which hasn't become a skyscraper yet,
and write my nostalgia through the lens.

Shanghai Transforming
Juan de Dios Perez

In the summer of 2005 I traveled with the architect Iker Gil to Shanghai to take photographs for this book. From the beginning I thought that his proposal to capture the transformation of the city was interesting, since it is a place that holds a special place in our minds: both exotic and mysterious.

But the reality of contemporary Shanghai, deprived of exotism and mystery, can only be described in numbers: seventeen million inhabitants, more than 4,000 skyscrapers reaching up to the 468 meter Oriental Pearl Tower. Shanghai's growth is so spectacular that the city map is renewed every six months. Neighborhoods disappear under the rubble, and with them, their inhabitants' histories.

Discovering Shanghai dramatically changed my idea of architecture and its relationship to us as human beings. Suddenly, I was face to face with the paradox of tranforming a city not to live in, but rather into an aesthetic object and symbol of economic power. Shanghai is a city created for admiration, and it seduces you from the moment you first set eyes on it. Appearing as a theme park, its grandiose and shiny architecture demands being observed and photographed.

However, I feel that with each change, this city loses more of its human dimension, and becomes increasingly detached from the idea of creating public space where people can relate to one another and live together. Shanghai today of this ideal. Shanghai shows its grief as a city full of empty spaces and walls. I reflect these solitary and contradictory places in my pictures with the hope of transmiting some of the feelings this city brought me.

Juan de Dios Perez

Shanghai Back Lot
Greg Girard

Apart from the central districts of the former French and International Concessions, Shanghai looks pretty much like every other city in China. However, to be fair, that's like saying New York, apart from Manhattan, looks like any other city in the US.

The Shanghai of the early-twentieth century was preserved for decades by a kind of benign neglect. For forty years following Mao's victory in 1949, Shanghai experienced no urban development for profit—none of the usual capitalistic churn that over time adds and removes features of the physical city.

Not until the early 1990s when Deng Xiaoping directed Shanghai to "catch up" (with southern cities like Shenzhen where economic reforms had transformed that city from a farming community to a manufacturing and administrative centre) did the city start to make itself modern again.

Since then, Shanghai has made up for lost time with a vengeance. Today no directives are required as developers compete to demolish or restore the remaining finite number of early-twentieth century neighborhoods and buildings.

As these neighborhoods and buildings gradually disappear, the city has provided film-makers looking for period Shanghai locations with a recreated 1930s version of itself on the outskirts of town. Known to industry insiders as the "Shanghai Back Lot," an official brochure for the place calls itself the "Shanghai Film and TV Amusement Park." When a production is underway actors and extras stroll on Nanjing Road between full-size replicas of actual buildings, and a lone streetcar runs back and forth on its two blocks of track.

Close-Up: Shanghai?
Jonathan Miller

My giant goes with me wherever I go.
—Emerson

Notes of a Virtual Adventurer

The elevator doors open in an office building in downtown Chicago, and across the hall, I glimpse a poster, taped on the glass window of a travel agent's office. It advertises an airline's flights to Shanghai with a view of gleaming skyscrapers at night and headlines the city as "Pearl of the Orient." Before I can discern whether I'm looking at the world of the future or the city of today, the elevator doors close.

The doors opening and closing on the image turn the elevator into a very special travel agent: a time machine.

As a film critic, I'm often whisked away to other times and places by the virtual voyages and imaginary caravans of the movie screen. In a way, the elevator simulates the cinema: images appear and disappear with the opening and closing of a shutter.

The doors close and off I go: to where and when? Travelers always have time for a bit of reflection while en route, some reading, or daydreaming, gazing distractedly on the panoramic scenes flitting past.

Establishing Shot

Many films open with a shot of a city or sequences of urban images to contextualize the coming drama. The opening images of Luis Buñuel's *Los Olvidados* (1950) exemplify how cinema returns to familiar monuments as shorthand indicators of particular cities. The film commences with a narrator speaking of "pits of misery" that are hidden behind "the imposing structures of our great modern cities" as shots of well-known landmarks appear on screen: the Eiffel Tower means Paris; Big Ben, London; Battery Park, New York. The part becomes the whole: the icon becomes the city.

Shanghai's skyline has played this role. The second shot of Steven Spielberg's 1987 film *Empire of the Sun*—an adaptation of author J.G. Ballard's fictionalized memoir of his boyhood during World War Two—offers a telephoto view of some of the Bund's classic skyscrapers. The landmark buildings (built in a variety of western styles) immediately conjure the historical city. Zhang Yimou's 1995 film *Shanghai Triad* is a romantic replication of Shanghai's 1930s gangster milieu. To bring the past to life, Zhang used period fashions, vintage cars and one long shot of the Bund.

Shanghai's image is not just a one-way street to the past. It can also bring the future to life. Recounting the long gestation of *Empire of the Sun*, J.G. Ballard described his recollection of 1930s Shanghai: "During the 1960s, the Shanghai of my childhood seemed a portent of the media cities of the future, dominated by advertising and mass circulation newspapers and swept by unpredictable violence."[1] In lieu of the media cities of the future, the city of today suffices. Not long ago Tokyo was the Asian city of choice for filmmakers in search of a futuristic urban frontier. Shanghai now makes the A-list for this role: a pin-up displaying all the charms of globalization.

1 — J.G. Ballard, "Look Back at Empire," *Guardian*, Saturday, March 4, 2006.

In Michael Winterbottom's 2003 film *Code 46*, Shanghai's newest architecture was casted as the backdrop to a near-distant surveillance society that monitors and controls the movements of both people and their DNA. A man and a woman who meet by chance (played by Tim Robbins and Samantha Morton) play out an ill-fated romance. Similarities in their gene sequences prevent their union, but something else also keeps them apart. The mannered narrative depends on a credible erotic spark between the two actors—which they do not generate. Ultimately, Shanghai's vibrant architecture gives the best performance.

In these and other films, the buildings of Shanghai's skyline—whether the Bund's "postcard collection of...colonial remains"[2] or freshly minted twenty-first-century skyscrapers—join a select group of structures that do service as efficient icons of complex realities.

Charm of Shanghai

Another postcard collection: in Shenzhen, China, at a theme park named "Windows on the World," scale models of the world's monuments jostle one another— vying for tourists' attention. Here, architecture crowds into a run-on sentence: "Today I saw the Eiffel Tower, the Tower of London, the Taj Mahal, the Empire State Building, the White House and...I forget them all, but I took lots of pictures." This architectural hit-parade occurs at other sites. At Legoland in California, world-famous buildings are made of the familiar plastic blocks, as if from some universal substance.

Architecture becomes a souvenir: a lovely charm bracelet of miniature buildings. Because the charms need only be images, we don't have to seek out these symptomatic displays; they come to us. True for the part and for the whole: cities circulate.

There was a time when travel was the primary way to confirm the character of a place. Writing of the influence photography exerted on art in the nineteenth-century, Aaron Scharf noted that

> many apparently authentic paintings of the Near East had previously been executed though the artists had never been within 1,000 miles of their subjects. This point is made in a letter of 1841 sent from Alexandria by the painter, Sir David Wilkie: "My object in this voyage was to see what has formed the scenes of so many pictures—the scenes of so many subjects painted from Scripture, but which have never been seen by the painters who have delineated them."[3]

Virtual cities can prompt an explorer to journey to see a fabled place with his or her own eyes. Imagination has been the true leader of every voyage of exploration. The first step toward El Dorado is the dream that it exists.

2 — Zhang Zhen, *An Amorous History of the Silver Screen: Chinese Cinema, 1896–1937* (Chicago: University of Chicago Press, 2005), 50.
3 — Aaron Scharf, *Art and Photography* (Baltimore: Penguin Books, 1974), 9.

Jonathan Miller

Although the world has shrunk since Wilkie's voyage, I don't know when I'll get to see Shanghai with my own eyes. Nonetheless, my curiosity piqued by the seductive logic of the travel poster, I wonder about the Shanghai that has formed the scene of so many pictures. For the moment, I'll have to rely on travel agents and time machines—elevators and motion pictures—to be my "Windows on the World."

A Close Look at the Urge to be Far Away

Differentiating places from the posters that advertise them presents an ongoing challenge, given our predilection to substitute iconic images for complex realities. Even fictional characters have had to confront the task of sorting out these intermingled geographies. Josef von Sternberg's 1941 film *The Shanghai Gesture* is swank pulp, stereotypical soundstage exoticism and atmospheric melodrama. In the film, a rich young society girl, Victoria Charteris, a.k.a. Poppy Smith, (played by Gene Tierney) goes looking for kicks in Shanghai. Poppy lands in Mother Gin Sling's Casino, where souls are clearly at stake since the set design—of descending circular levels—calls to mind the "pits of misery" of Dante's *Inferno*. Von Sternberg's film was based upon a play by John Colton that caused a stir for its frank presentation of sexuality when it ran on Broadway in 1926 (the original setting—a brothel—was too lurid for Hollywood even at the time of adaptation, and necessitated the switch from bordello to casino). The stimulating atmosphere in Shanghai's night-world inferno overwhelms Poppy: "I didn't think such a place existed, except in my own imagination. It has a ghastly familiarity like a half-remembered dream.... Anything could happen here."

Becoming accustomed to the image in lieu of the actuality imparts a perplexing impact when the long-imagined thing itself is finally seen. Sometimes it surprises and sometimes it disappoints, as writer Georges Perec registered in *Species of Spaces and Other Pieces*. Still, the urge to be far away drives desire:

> To see something *in reality* that had long been an image in an old dictionary: a geyser, a waterfall, the Bay of Naples, the spot where Gavrilo Princip was standing when he shot at Archduke Franz-Ferdinand of Austria and Duchess Sophia of Hohenberg, on the corner of Franz-Josef Street and the Appel Quay in Sarajevo, just opposite the Simic Brothers' bar on 28 June 1914, at 11.15 a.m.[4]

Zeroing in on the spatio-temporal specifics of a historical event, Perec makes it clear how we rely on places to function as signposts, arrows pointing out the imaginary route from the here and now to the here and then.

For most of us, the opportunity to see something in reality does not come easily, if at all. Still, the desire can be slaked somewhat by substitutes. We can visit the apparently authentic Shanghai of representations by browsing images in Perec's "old dictionary," or seeing the city on screen.

4 — Georges Perec, *Species of Spaces and Other Pieces* (London: Penguin Books, 1977), 77.

Ghost Naming Place

In cities, because the past subsists in the present, the invisible coexists with the visible. As we look at the actual city, its phantom counterpart takes shape. ("He was standing there, right there, when he shot the Archduke!") As Michel de Certeau describes, places are haunted by spectral presences: names of things that used to be, events that happened there once.

> What can be seen designates what is no longer there: "you *see*, here there used to be...," but it can no longer be seen. Demonstratives indicate the invisible identities of the visible: it is the very definition of a place, in fact, that it is composed by these series of displacements and effect among them fragmented strata that form it and that it plays on these moving layers.[5]

Informed by de Certeau, film scholar Zhang Zhen recounts the experience of Shanghai in recent years as traversing a city in flux. Her Shanghai is a haunted, dynamic and layered profusion of signs in which names chart time:

> How ironic that the Paris Theater on Huaihai Road...is now the site of a chic commercial building called Times Square. It's not clear whether it is intended as a memorial of the bygone years or a hymn to the breathlessly hectic present in the former French concession.[6]

We shunt aside the past to make way for an all-engulfing moment of new and now. The "invisible identities of the visible" find refuge in the substance of the city, imbuing its cracks and shadows, persisting in a random archive of fading memories, hiding behind official monuments , and encoded in overdetermined fictions. In this view, the present and the past coexist in a composition of "fragmented and , displaced strata."

Defining a place as a residue of displacements makes it akin to the protagonist of a drama, one who confronts her true identity when unpaid debts from the past get settled... The elevator doors open: back at Mother Gin Sling's Casino.

Flowers of Shanghai

Poor Poppy. She hooks up with Doctor Omar, an opportunistic go-between played by Victor Mature who does Mother Gin Sling's bidding and spiels poetic wisdom with the sagacity of a fortune cookie. Poppy gets hooked on gambling and drink, pawns her jewels to fuel her habit, becomes indebted to Mother Gin Sling, and moving quickly from virtue to vice, finds that Shanghai is no amusement park. Elevator going down.

Two famous Hollywood films linked to Shanghai, Josef von Sternberg's *The Shanghai Express* (1932) and Orson Welles's *The Lady from Shanghai* (1947) lack Shanghai landmarks. Using other means to evoke place, they illustrate the roles the city has played in the Western imagination.

5 — Michel de Certeau, *The Practice of Everyday Life* (Berkeley: University of California Press, 1988), 108.
6 — Zhang, *An Amorous History*, 34.

Jonathan Miller

Von Sternberg's film takes place on the titular train ride, ending at the station in Shanghai (or a Hollywood back-lot version of it). Marlene Dietrich stars as one of the passengers— the infamous "white flower of the China coast"—Shanghai Lily. Accounting for her reputation, Dietrich's character declares in a famous line that "It took more than one man to change my name to Shanghai Lily." According to the conventions of the era, filmgoers knew immediately and unequivocally what this meant. Critic Roger Dooley suggest that

> possibly in consequence of the lurid reputation of the play *The Shanghai Gesture*, the very name of the city, like those of Singapore and Panama, had become a code word for vice. A character who called herself Shanghai Mae, Panama Flor or Singapore Sal announced her profession with her name.[7]

Shanghai Lily, Poppy Smith and others carry the burden of the city's name as a sign of unshakeable histories. On this train ride, Lily happens to meet the man she once loved, Captain Donald "Doc" Harvey, played by Clive Brook. By dint of an act of self-sacrifice, she proves her moral character to him, and this time he doesn't let true love slip away. Lily redeems herself and resumes her real name: Magdalene.

Dietrich's Shanghai Lily could have crossed paths with another white flower: Elsa Bannister, the *Lady from Shanghai* played by Rita Hayworth in Orson Welles's film. Starting in New York, and traveling via yacht to San Francisco, the story doesn't take place in China at all. That the lady is from Shanghai indicates she has an unresolved, immoral past. She too is composed of displaced, fragmented strata. When she meets Michael O'Hara, the character played by Welles, she alludes to her birth in China, and, of time spent in Shanghai, declares: "You need more than luck in Shanghai."

To need more than luck means one has to create one's fate, whatever it takes. Because of her Shanghai history, Elsa Bannister is an experienced schemer. Here, the city is equated with capability and becomes a clue to her manipulative drive. More than a memory or locale, it's a set of skills: a *savoir-faire*. Elsa speaks Chinese (*savoir-dire*) and, moreover, she's capable of the sort of intricate intrigue that the word 'Shanghai' has historically connoted. Elsa Bannister is another of Welles's characters whose actions prove their immutable character.

But is a city's character unalterable? Surely Shanghai no longer functions as cosmopolitan mark of shame as it did in the early decades of the last century. What changed Shanghai from a code word for vice to one for twenty-first-century, cutting-edge urbanity?

7 — Roger Dooley, *From Scarface to Scarlett: American Films in the 1930s* (New York: Harvest / Harcourt Brace Jovanovich, 1981), 5.

All About Shanghai

A 1930s guidebook, *All About Shanghai*, declared Shanghai "...the most cosmopolitan city on the world, the fishing village on a mudflat which almost literally overnight became a great metropolis." [8] Given the present pace of urbanization in China, it seems nothing can keep a city from springing up overnight as many times as it pleases.

After naming it the "Paris of the Orient," the same guidebook described Shanghai as the "New York of the West." When cities are compared to one another, magnitude means mastery. Personified as agonistic competitors, they duel for bragging rights and record books. Beijing swallows three Manhattans in preparation for the 2008 Olympics.[9] By no means out of the race, Shanghai shoots "for the top as it ascends the hierarchy of world cities, with one eye on longtime champions like New York, and another on its fraternal rival, Beijing." [10] Shanghai already has lapped New York in the skyscraper race.[11]

The day may come when New York will be known as a Shanghai-wannabe of the past. Just as in the 1950 film *All About Eve,* the understudy becomes the star.

Miller's Haunted Bund

In 1978 playwright Arthur Miller and his wife, photographer Inge Morath, traveled in China. In *Chinese Encounters*—the collaborative travelogue that resulted—Miller recounted their experiences in the immediate post-Mao period. The momentum that now drives the phenomenal development of Shanghai and other Chinese cities was just beginning to gather.

In Shanghai, Miller stayed in a hotel on the Bund. He detailed a moment's reverie as he looked out of the window at the city.

> I stared down at a street of once elegant shops, now dismally empty, that had carried some of the most elegant clothes and expensive luggage and jewelry in the world. The drizzle may have helped but in its snug architectural tone the quarter was reminiscent of London's Mayfair around Dorchester Hotel and cosseting Mount Street, and it was not at all difficult to imagine the Rolls and Bentleys and Delahayes driving up and the golden lasses stepping out to join for luncheon the cheery young gentlemen through whose hand the cargoes in the harbor passed and left behind percentages.[12]

The lively urbanity of Shanghai in the early-twentieth-century persists for the dramatic imagination. A real history gives rise to the vision which then takes on a life of its own, and Miller's imagined scene reminds us that a city is a place where ghosts are always at large.

8 — From Zhang, *An Amorous History*, 42.
9 — Anne-Marie Broudehoux, "Delirious Beijing: Euphoria and Despair in the Olympic Metropolis" in *Evil Paradises: Dream Worlds of Neoliberalism*, (New York: The New Press, 2007), 88.
10 — Howard French, "Shanghai's Boom: A Building Frenzy," *New York Times*, Thursday, April 13, 2006.
11 — "Shanghai Urban Development: The Future Is Now," *Morning Edition*, NPR, December 11, 2006.
12 — Arthur Miller and Inge Morath, *Chinese Encounters* (New York: Farrar, Straus and Giroux, 1979), 107.

See the Future in a Handful of Rice

For Miller, the empty communist street evoked the ghost of a capitalist and colonialist one: bustling with golden, cheery Westerners. Now, China's full streets keep filling up, and the hyperventilating bustle of consumer culture pushes old ghosts aside or immures them in quaintly tailored shopping districts. Globalization paves over the local and historical to make way for a ubiquitous present. Ghosts, and their haunting places, get pushed to the threshold of a final disappearance.

Miller's perspective as world-famous first-worlder (at one time as iconic as the Manhattan skyline) allowed him the luxury to express discontent with the material blandishments of the West. He surprised his Chinese companions by admitting that happiness is not a necessary product of wealth. The existential dilemma made no sense to the Chinese who did not lack a *raison d'être*. For them, it was a simple equation: "the reason we live is to build up our country." Miller kept his doubts to himself, but considered what was being discussed an "accomplishment so distant in time... that there was no reality in thinking beyond it." [13]

Miller might as well have been Sam Salt, the American gambler played by bullfrog-voiced Eugene Pallette in *Shanghai Express*, who declares, "What future is there in being a Chinaman? You're born, eat your way through a handful of rice and ya die." Nowadays, the future has emigrated: it resides in China. Miller's inability to imagine the country "built-up" points to more than a failure of prediction. It is symptomatic of an endemic shortsightedness.

Perhaps Miller couldn't see how China would transform itself due to an inevitable tendency for Westerners to think about the East in ahistorical terms and defined by a set of pre-existing tropes. The American mainstream cinema has created, mirrored, and amplified popular cultural attitudes about China, concocting it out of a narrow range of ingredients: exoticism, sexuality, inscrutability, viciousness, sophistication and primitivity. Mass media have perpetuated the dissemination of this static conception, as Edward Said noted:

> One aspect of the electronic, postmodern world is that there has been a rein-
> forcement of the stereotypes by which the Orient is viewed. Television, the films
> and all the media's resources have forced information into more and more stan-
> dardized molds. So far as the Orient is concerned, standardization and cultural
> stereotyping have intensified the hold of the nineteenth-century academic and
> imaginative demonology of "the mysterious Orient." [14]

Whether or not the hold of this "demonology" has relaxed since Said wrote the above statement, standardized molds continue to shape the images of China we consume, and stereotypes continue to be pervasive as vehicles for cultural attitudes.

13 — Ibid, 107.
14 — Edward Said, *Orientalism* (New York: Vintage Books, 1979), 24.

The travel poster that dubs Shanghai "Pearl of the Orient," overwrites the implicit colonialism of the Modern-era nickname "Paris of the Orient." In the process, it demonstrates how information gets crammed into ready-made molds. Moreover, the new tag sounds ambiguous. As it advertises vanguard urbanity, does it occult something else? As the signifiers start to slip, other connotations crop up: lustrous, feminine, "Pearl of the Orient"—it's hard to avoid wondering whether she might have worked with Shanghai Lily.

City at Night

French poet and diplomat Paul Claudel described Shanghai in *Connaissance de l'Est,* his collection of prose poems written in 1896 while he served as French vice-consul to China. In one, *The City at Night,* Claudel sought to define Shanghai's singular identity:

> If we seek the explanation, the reason why this city through which we make our way is so completely distinct among all our crowded memories, we are at once struck by a fact: there are no horses in the streets. The city is entirely human. The Chinese hold as a manner of principle that animal or machine assistance is not to be used for a task by which a man can live. This explains the narrowness of the streets, the stairs, the curved bridges, the houses without fences, the winding alleys and passages. The city forms a coherent whole, an industrious mixture interconnected in all its parts, perforated like an ant-hill... The broad streets necessary for the rapid general traffic of a simplified mechanical existence would find no place here.[15]

The Shanghai through which Claudel made his way no longer coheres. It shimmers now as a spectral presence, haunting the edges of the imagination. Filmmaker Hou Hsiao-hsien gives this city dimension in his exquisite 1998 film *Flowers of Shanghai.* The drama takes place in the late nineteenth century inside one of Shanghai's elegant brothels or "Flower Houses." There are no exteriors, no long shots of yet-to-be-built Bund skyscrapers: this is a Shanghai of interiors and manners, where the vicissitudes of passion are at odds with the constraints of a strict social order; thus ultimately, beyond virtue and vice—a fundamentally modern place.

The "rapid general traffic of a simplified mechanical existence" swallows up Shanghai's narrow streets and alleys. Technological and economic developments sweep away the city where human facts once determined existence. Here as elsewhere, as the "entirely human" city becomes a memory, it simultaneously looms on the horizon as an ideal. The more skyscrapers built, the more neighborhoods razed, the more ghosts. An urban condition that actively promotes the dignity, potential, and creativity of its residents is an alluring and elusive vision. Yet sprawling, inhumane development will ensure that it remains an image.

15 — Paul Claudel, *Knowing the East* (Princeton, Princeton University Press, 2004), 10.

Jonathan Miller

Mapping New Glitter

A multi-faceted sign—the shiniest new charm on a bracelet of urban icons—Shanghai will transform dynamically as the actual city grows and the world grapples with Chinese development. One glimpse through opening elevator doors won't suffice to describe how the rapidly evolving city's image will travel around the globe, or what pits of misery are hidden behind its façade.

Shanghai as emblem of mysterious Orientalism flickers into the past without fading from view. Snapping into focus in the foreground is a Shanghai that turns the twentieth-century metropolis into a rough first draft. Today—and tomorrow—Shanghai produces a new cityscape for the imagination. The contour of the city's image gets actively remapped and the "glittering lights of the concession" that once dazzled Claudel morph into the blazing electronic skyline of this incomparable twenty-first century metropolis. We virtual adventurers can hope to see with our own eyes what has formed the scene of so many pictures—the actual city, Shanghai, its skies untainted by clouds of irreversible blight.

Social Transformation

Administrative Divisions Population
2005

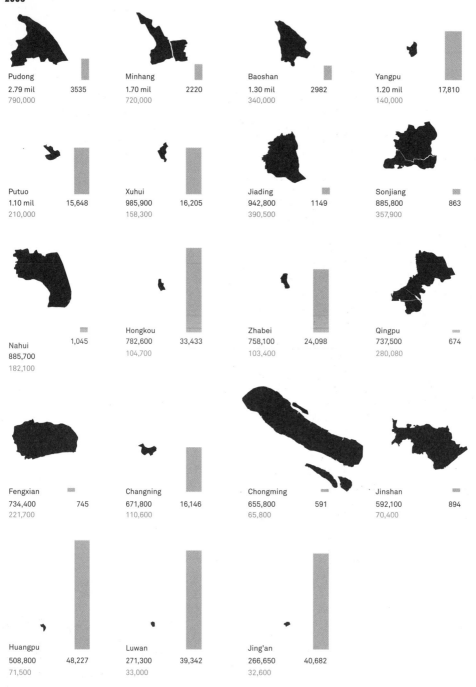

Pudong	Minhang	Baoshan	Yangpu
2.79 mil 3535	1.70 mil 2220	1.30 mil 2982	1.20 mil 17,810
790,000	720,000	340,000	140,000

Putuo	Xuhui	Jiading	Sonjiang
1.10 mil 15,648	985,900 16,205	942,800 1149	885,800 863
210,000	158,300	390,500	357,900

Nahui	Hongkou	Zhabei	Qingpu
1,045	782,600 33,433	758,100 24,098	737,500 674
Nahui 885,700	104,700	103,400	280,080
182,100			

Fengxian	Changning	Chongming	Jinshan
734,400 745	671,800 16,146	655,800 591	592,100 894
221,700	110,600	65,800	70,400

Huangpu	Luwan	Jing'an
508,800 48,227	271,300 39,342	266,650 40,682
71,500	33,000	32,600

province

density

population (person/km²)

floating population

Source: *Shanghai Statistical Yearbook 2006*. Shanghai Municipal Statistics Bureau.
(Beijing: China Statistics Press, 2006) Table 3.3.

Resident Population refers to the population that actually reside in a place (residence) permanently usually longer than half a year.
Floating Population refers to the population with registration in the police

International Settlement

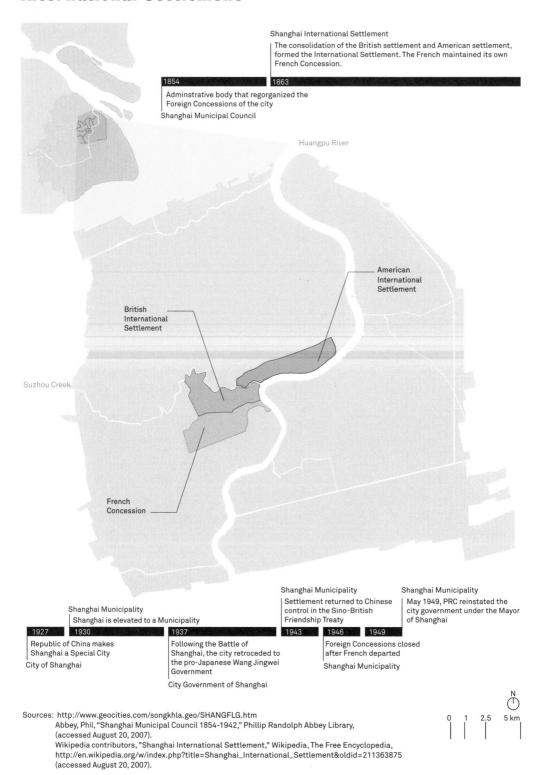

Shanghai International Settlement

The consolidation of the British settlement and American settlement, formed the International Settlement. The French maintained its own French Concession.

| 1854 | 1863 |

Adminstrative body that regorganized the Foreign Concessions of the city

Shanghai Municipal Council

Huangpu River

American International Settlement

British International Settlement

Suzhou Creek

French Concession

Shanghai Municipality
Settlement returned to Chinese control in the Sino-British Friendship Treaty

Shanghai Municipality
May 1949, PRC reinstated the city government under the Mayor of Shanghai

Shanghai Municipality
Shanghai is elevated to a Municipality

| 1927 | 1930 | 1937 | 1943 | 1946 | 1949 |

Republic of China makes Shanghai a Special City

City of Shanghai

Following the Battle of Shanghai, the city retroceded to the pro-Japanese Wang Jingwei Government

City Government of Shanghai

Foreign Concessions closed after French departed

Shanghai Municipality

N

0   1   2.5   5 km

Sources: http://www.geocities.com/songkhla.geo/SHANGFLG.htm
     Abbey, Phil, "Shanghai Municipal Council 1854-1942," Phillip Randolph Abbey Library, (accessed August 20, 2007).
     Wikipedia contributors, "Shanghai International Settlement," Wikipedia, The Free Encyclopedia, http://en.wikipedia.org/w/index.php?title=Shanghai_International_Settlement&oldid=211363875 (accessed August 20, 2007).

Historical Population
1980-2005

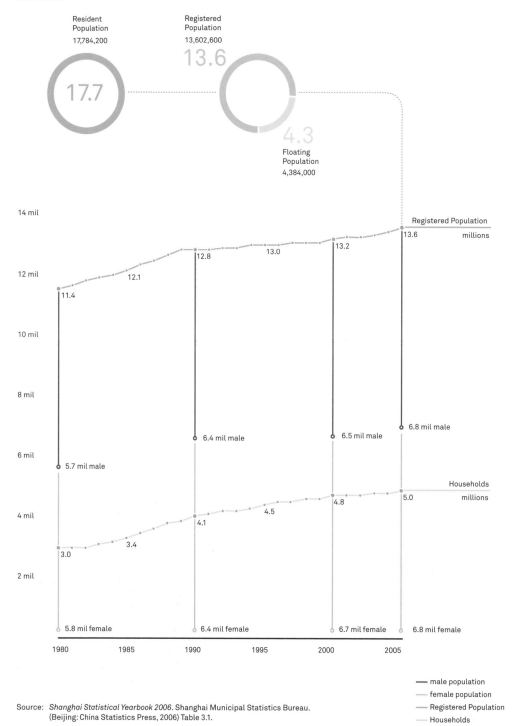

Resident Population
17,784,200

Registered Population
13,602,600

13.6

17.7

4.3

Floating Population
4,384,000

Registered Population
13.6
millions

14 mil

12 mil

11.4

12.1

12.8

13.0

13.2

10 mil

8 mil

6.4 mil male

6.5 mil male

6.8 mil male

6 mil

5.7 mil male

Households
5.0
millions

4.1

4.5

4.8

4 mil

3.0

3.4

2 mil

5.8 mil female

6.4 mil female

6.7 mil female

6.8 mil female

1980   1985   1990   1995   2000   2005

— male population
— female population
— Registered Population
— Households

Source: *Shanghai Statistical Yearbook 2006*. Shanghai Municipal Statistics Bureau.
          (Beijing: China Statistics Press, 2006) Table 3.1.

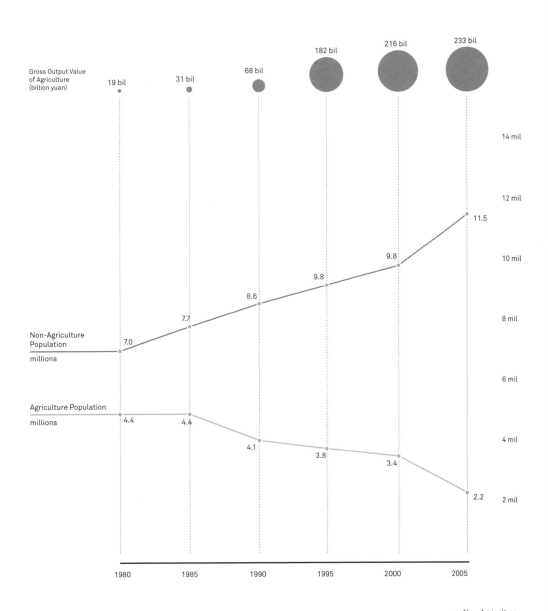

Gross Output Value
of Agriculture
(billion yuan)

19 bil   31 bil   68 bil   182 bil   216 bil   233 bil

14 mil

12 mil

11.5

9.8

10 mil

9.8

8.6

8 mil

7.7

Non-Agriculture
Population
millions   7.0

6 mil

Agriculture Population
millions   4.4   4.4

4.1   4 mil

3.8

3.4

2.2   2 mil

1980   1985   1990   1995   2000   2005

— Non-Agriculture
Population
— Agriculture
Population

Source: *Shanghai Statistical Yearbook 2006*. Shanghai Municipal Statistics Bureau.
(Beijing: China Statistics Press, 2006) Table 3.1, 12.1.

China Administrative Divisions Population
2005

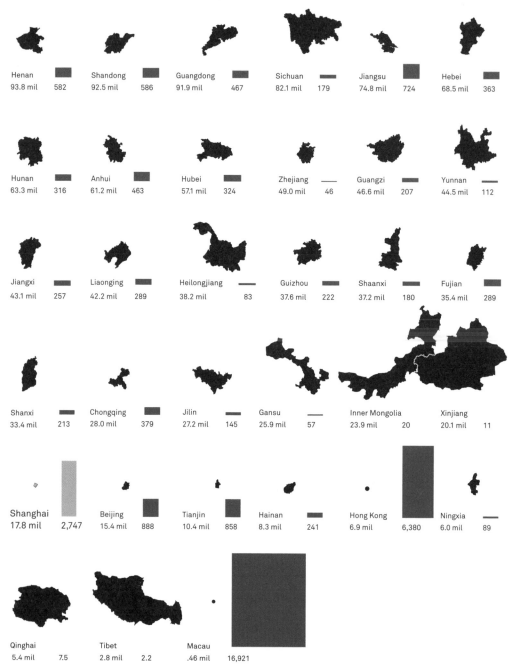

Province	Population	Density
Henan	93.8 mil	582
Shandong	92.5 mil	586
Guangdong	91.9 mil	467
Sichuan	82.1 mil	179
Jiangsu	74.8 mil	724
Hebei	68.5 mil	363
Hunan	63.3 mil	316
Anhui	61.2 mil	463
Hubei	57.1 mil	324
Zhejiang	49.0 mil	46
Guangzi	46.6 mil	207
Yunnan	44.5 mil	112
Jiangxi	43.1 mil	257
Liaoning	42.2 mil	289
Heilongjiang	38.2 mil	83
Guizhou	37.6 mil	222
Shaanxi	37.2 mil	180
Fujian	35.4 mil	289
Shanxi	33.4 mil	213
Chongqing	28.0 mil	379
Jilin	27.2 mil	145
Gansu	25.9 mil	57
Inner Mongolia	23.9 mil	20
Xinjiang	20.1 mil	11
Shanghai	17.8 mil	2,747
Beijing	15.4 mil	888
Tianjin	10.4 mil	858
Hainan	8.3 mil	241
Hong Kong	6.9 mil	6,380
Ningxia	6.0 mil	89
Qinghai	5.4 mil	7.5
Tibet	2.8 mil	2.2
Macau	.46 mil	16,921

Sources: *China Statistical Yearbook 2006*. National Bureau of Statistics of China
(Beijing: China Statistics Press, 2006) Table 4.1, 4.2, 4.03.
United Nations World Urbanization Prospects: The 2007 Revision Population Database
http://esa.un.org/unup

province
population   density
(person/km²)

China Historical Population

1980-2005

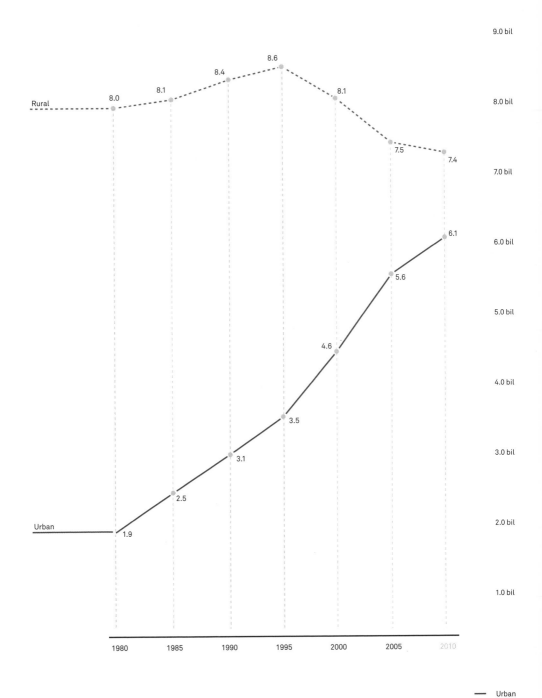

Rural

8.0   8.1   8.4   8.6   8.1   7.5   7.4

6.1

5.6

4.6

3.5

3.1

2.5

Urban

1.9

9.0 bil

8.0 bil

7.0 bil

6.0 bil

5.0 bil

4.0 bil

3.0 bil

2.0 bil

1.0 bil

1980   1985   1990   1995   2000   2005   2010

—— Urban

--- Rural

(excluding Hong kong SAR, Macao SAR, and Taiwan Province)

Urban and Rural Household

1990-2005

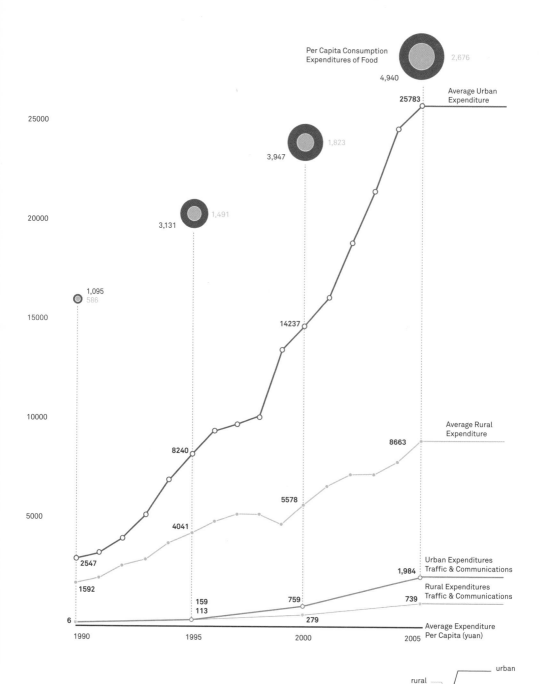

Per Capita Consumption
Expenditures of Food

2,676

4,940

Average Urban
Expenditure

25783

1,823

3,947

3,131

1,491

1,095
586

Average Rural
Expenditure

14237

8663

8240

4041

5578

Urban Expenditures
Traffic & Communications

2547

1,984

1592

Rural Expenditures
Traffic & Communications

159
113

759

739

6

279

Average Expenditure
Per Capita (yuan)

25000

20000

15000

10000

5000

1990   1995   2000   2005

urban

rural

= in yuan

Source: *Shanghai Statistical Yearbook 2006*. Shanghai Municipal Statistics Bureau.
(Beijing: China Statistics Press, 2006) Table 10.14, 10.18.

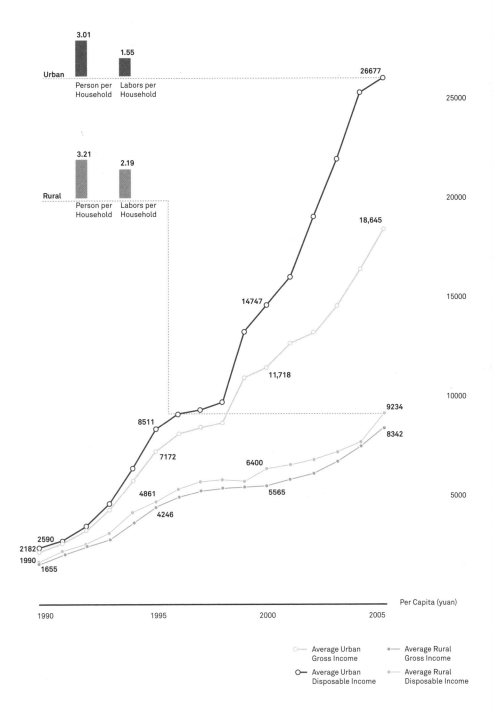

Urban

3.01
Person per
Household

1.55
Labors per
Household

Rural

3.21
Person per
Household

2.19
Labors per
Household

26677

25000

18,645

20000

14747

15000

11,718

8511

10000

9234

8342

7172

6400

4861

5565

4246

5000

2590
2182
1990
1655

Per Capita (yuan)

1990   1995   2000   2005

○— Average Urban   ●— Average Rural
Gross Income   Gross Income

O— Average Urban   ●— Average Rural
Disposable Income   Disposable Income

Population Age
2005

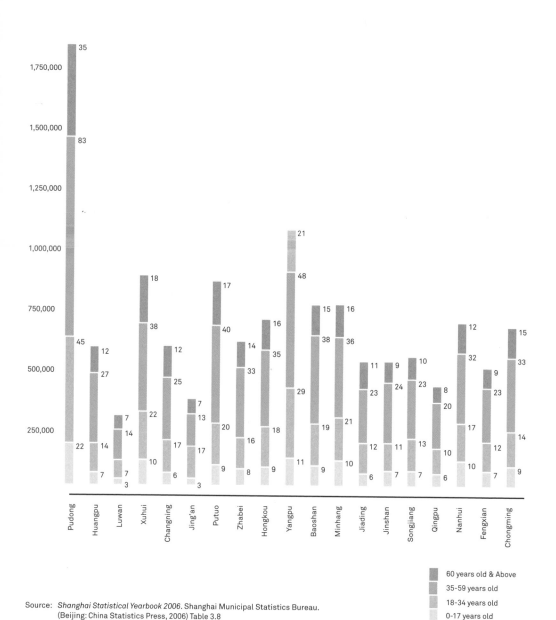

Source: *Shanghai Statistical Yearbook 2006*. Shanghai Municipal Statistics Bureau.
(Beijing: China Statistics Press, 2006) Table 3.8

Legend:
- 60 years old & Above
- 35-59 years old
- 18-34 years old
- 0-17 years old

Birthrate
1980-2005

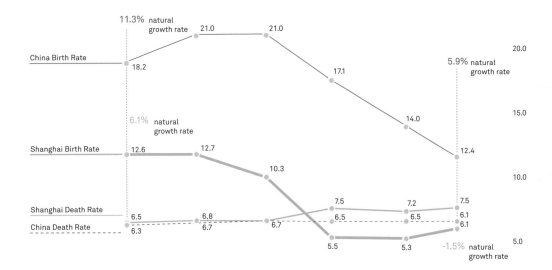

11.3% natural growth rate

China Birth Rate — 18.2 | 21.0 | 21.0 | 17.1 | 14.0 | 12.4

5.9% natural growth rate

6.1% natural growth rate

Shanghai Birth Rate — 12.6 | 12.7 | 10.3

Shanghai Death Rate — 6.5 | 6.8 | 7.5 | 7.2 | 7.5
China Death Rate — 6.3 | 6.7 | 6.7 | 6.5 | 6.5 | 6.1 | 6.1

5.5 | 5.3

-1.5% natural growth rate

20.0
15.0
10.0
5.0

Birth & Death Rate %

1980   1985   1990   1995   2000   2005

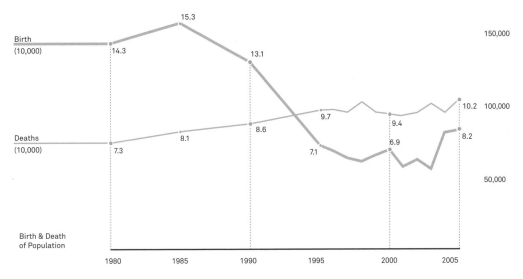

Birth (10,000) — 14.3 | 15.3 | 13.1 | 7.1 | 6.9 | 8.2

Deaths (10,000) — 7.3 | 8.1 | 8.6 | 9.7 | 9.4 | 10.2

150,000
100,000
50,000

Birth & Death of Population

1980   1985   1990   1995   2000   2005

— China Birth Rate
--- China Death Rate
▬ Shanghai Birth
— Shanghai Death

Sources: *Shanghai Statistical Yearbook 2006*. Shanghai Municipal Statistics Bureau.
(Beijing: China Statistics Press, 2006) Table 3.4,
China Statistical Yearbook 2006. National Bureau of Statistics of China.,
(Beijing: China Statistics Press, 2006) Table 4.2.

Education Institutions

1980-2005

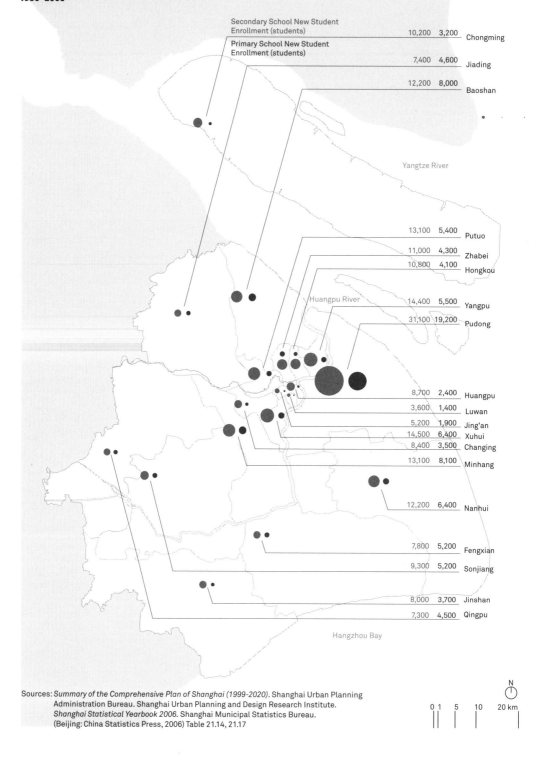

Secondary School New Student
Enrollment (students)

10,200	3,200	Chongming

Primary School New Student
Enrollment (students)

7,400	4,600	Jiading
12,200	8,000	Baoshan

Yangtze River

13,100	5,400	Putuo
11,000	4,300	Zhabei
10,800	4,100	Hongkou

Huangpu River

14,400	5,500	Yangpu
31,100	19,200	Pudong
8,700	2,400	Huangpu
3,600	1,400	Luwan
5,200	1,900	Jing'an
14,500	6,400	Xuhui
8,400	3,500	Changing
13,100	8,100	Minhang
12,200	6,400	Nanhui
7,800	5,200	Fengxian
9,300	5,200	Sonjiang
8,000	3,700	Jinshan
7,300	4,500	Qingpu

Hangzhou Bay

Sources: *Summary of the Comprehensive Plan of Shanghai (1999-2020)*. Shanghai Urban Planning
    Administration Bureau. Shanghai Urban Planning and Design Research Institute.
    Shanghai Statistical Yearbook 2006. Shanghai Municipal Statistics Bureau.
    (Beijing: China Statistics Press, 2006) Table 21.14, 21.17

N

0 1   5   10   20 km

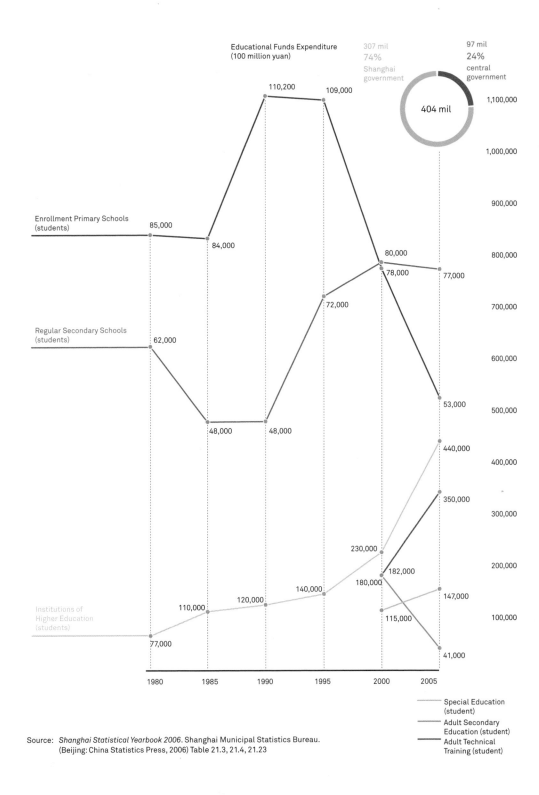

Educational Funds Expenditure
(100 million yuan)

307 mil
74%
Shanghai
government

97 mil
24%
central
government

404 mil

110,200

109,000

1,100,000

1,000,000

900,000

Enrollment Primary Schools
(students)

85,000

84,000

80,000
78,000

77,000

800,000

72,000

700,000

Regular Secondary Schools
(students)

62,000

600,000

53,000

500,000

48,000   48,000

440,000

400,000

350,000

300,000

230,000

182,000

200,000

Institutions of
Higher Education
(students)

140,000

120,000

110,000

180,000

147,000

115,000

100,000

77,000

41,000

1980   1985   1990   1995   2000   2005

——— Special Education
         (student)
——— Adult Secondary
         Education (student)
——— Adult Technical
         Training (student)

Source: *Shanghai Statistical Yearbook 2006*. Shanghai Municipal Statistics Bureau.
         (Beijing: China Statistics Press, 2006) Table 21.3, 21.4, 21.23

Publications
1980-2005

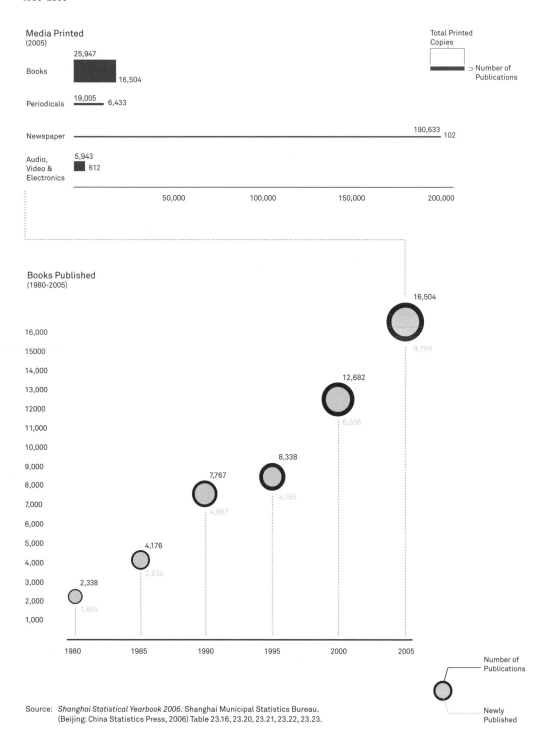

Media Printed
(2005)

Total Printed
Copies

⊐ Number of
Publications

Books
25,947
16,504

Periodicals
19,005
6,433

Newspaper
190,633
102

Audio,
Video &
Electronics
5,943
612

50,000   100,000   150,000   200,000

Books Published
(1980-2005)

16,504
9,286

16,000
15000
14,000
13,000
12000
11,000
10,000
9,000
8,000
7,000
6,000
5,000
4,000
3,000
2,000
1,000

12,682
6,936

8,338
4,185

7,767
4,887

4,176
2,634

2,338
1,804

1980   1985   1990   1995   2000   2005

Number of
Publications

Newly
Published

Source: *Shanghai Statistical Yearbook 2006.* Shanghai Municipal Statistics Bureau.
(Beijing: China Statistics Press, 2006) Table 23.16, 23.20, 23.21, 23.22, 23.23.

Television and Broadcasting Stations

2005

Cable Popularity Rate

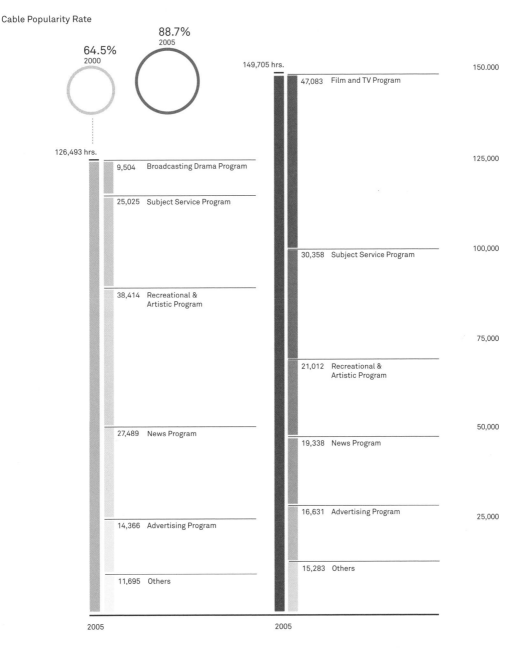

64.5%
2000

88.7%
2005

126,493 hrs.

149,705 hrs.

150.000

47,083   Film and TV Program

9,504   Broadcasting Drama Program

125,000

25,025   Subject Service Program

100,000

30,358   Subject Service Program

38,414   Recreational &
            Artistic Program

75,000

21,012   Recreational &
            Artistic Program

50,000

27,489   News Program

19,338   News Program

16,631   Advertising Program

25,000

14,366   Advertising Program

15,283   Others

11,695   Others

2005

2005

Total
Broadcasting Stations (hours)
Television Stations (hours)

Source: *Shanghai Statistical Yearbook 2006*. Shanghai Municipal Statistics Bureau.
          (Beijing: China Statistics Press, 2006) Table 23.8, 23.9, 23.10.

Telecommunications
2002-2005

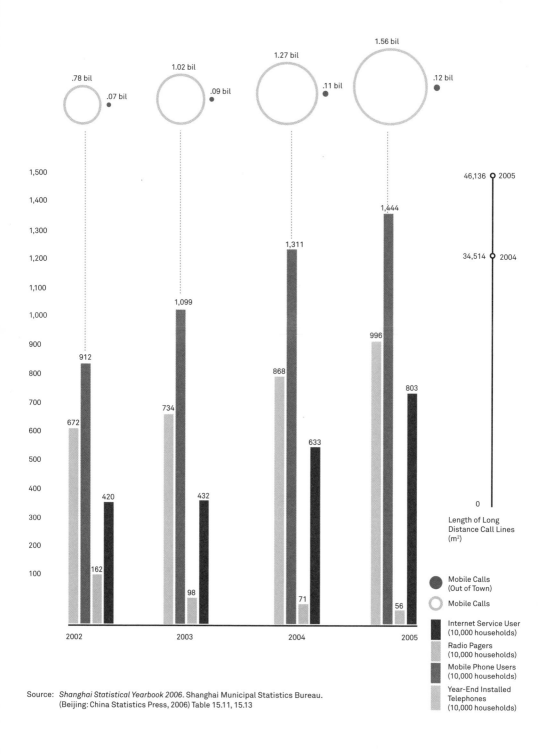

.78 bil   .07 bil   1.02 bil   .09 bil   1.27 bil   .11 bil   1.56 bil   .12 bil

1,500
1,400
1,300
1,200
1,100
1,000
900
800
700
600
500
400
300
200
100

2002   2003   2004   2005

672   912   162   420
734   1,099   98   432
868   1,311   71   633
996   1,444   56   803

1,444

46,136   2005

34,514   2004

0

Length of Long
Distance Call Lines
(m²)

● Mobile Calls
  (Out of Town)
○ Mobile Calls

■ Internet Service User
  (10,000 households)
■ Radio Pagers
  (10,000 households)
■ Mobile Phone Users
  (10,000 households)
■ Year-End Installed
  Telephones
  (10,000 households)

Source: *Shanghai Statistical Yearbook 2006*. Shanghai Municipal Statistics Bureau.
          (Beijing: China Statistics Press, 2006) Table 15.11, 15.13

China Internet Users by Administrative Division

2005

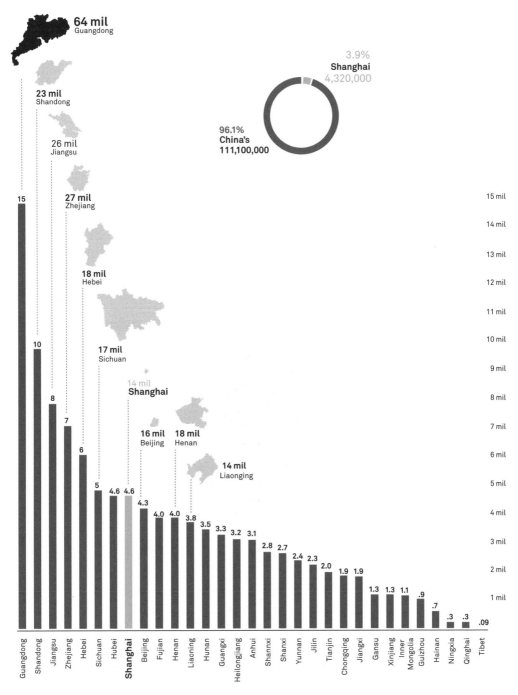

64 mil
Guangdong

23 mil
Shandong

26 mil
Jiangsu

27 mil
Zhejiang

18 mil
Hebei

17 mil
Sichuan

14 mil
Shanghai

16 mil
Beijing

18 mil
Henan

14 mil
Liaonging

3.9%
Shanghai
4,320,000

96.1%
China's
111,100,000

15	15 mil
	14 mil
	13 mil
	12 mil
10	11 mil
	10 mil
8	9 mil
7	8 mil
6	7 mil
5 4.6 4.6	6 mil
4.3	5 mil
4.0 4.0	4 mil
3.8 3.5 3.3 3.2 3.1	3 mil
2.8 2.7 2.4 2.3 2.0	2 mil
1.9 1.9 1.3 1.3 1.1	1 mil
.9 .7 .3 .3 .09	

Guangdong
Shandong
Jiangsu
Zhejiang
Hebei
Sichuan
Hubei
Shanghai
Beijing
Fujian
Henan
Liaoning
Hunan
Guangxi
Heilongjiang
Anhui
Shannxi
Shanxi
Yunnan
Jilin
Tianjin
Chongqing
Jiangxi
Gansu
Xinjiang
Inner Mongolia
Guizhou
Hainan
Ningxia
Qinghai
Tibet

Source: *China Statistical Yearbook 2006*. National Bureau of Statistics of China
(Beijing: China Statistics Press, 2006) Table 16.40.

The city's central area in the 1930s

From *Lilong* to International Community
Xiangning Li
Xiaochun Zhang

In *Street Angel* (1937), based on an American film of the same name, Shanghai was depicted as a flamboyant modern metropolis full of seductions, yet people from the lowest strata of society were confined in their shabby dwellings. Shanghai has long regarded itself as a paragon of integration of Eastern and Western civilizations and the embodiment of modern cosmopolitanism. Studying the housing models that have dominated its urban fabric at different times during the twentieth-century, however, reveals that the city has undergone an equally pronounced struggle to implement and maintain these ideals.

Pre-Revolution

Ever since Shanghai was forced open as a treaty port in 1843, there have been contests for urban space between the Chinese and the foreigners who have settled there. Entrepreneurs, merchants and landlords from neighboring areas of the city rushed into it during the latter half of the nineteenth-century because of the Opium War and the Peasants Uprising, and the city again experienced a surge in migrants in the early-twentieth-century due to the capitalist revolution and subsequent wars among warlords. These newcomers invested and conducted commercial activities in the foreign concessions, promoting the development of a real estate market and especially, a housing market.

From a bird's-eye view of Shanghai in the 1920s (aside from the high-rises of the Bund), the base of the urban fabric was the *lilong*: a mixture of Chinese and Western housing types. The Shaighainese *lilong* first appeared in the 1860s as a variation of the older Shikumen *lilong*, which is itself a variant of the traditional courtyard house commonly seen in southern China.

In the 1920s and 30s, four types of *Lilong* housing appeared: new-style Shikumen *lilong*, new-style *lilong*, garden *lilong*, apartment *lilong*. The new-style *lilong* was designed to address the changes that commercial developments had brought to Shanghai, consisting of a main lane and sublanes which resembled the structure of a fish skeleton. In addition to *Lilong* housing, during that period of time in Shanghai there were also single-family garden residences, urban apartments and shanty towns or slum houses.

At this time, factories were located along the Huangpu River and Suzhou Creek. Crude dormitories were constructed near them, and on the outskirts of foreign concessions. Lilong were instead constructed in the downtown area, and its surrounding neighborhood, accommodating more than half of Shanghai's inhabitants. In the concessions especially the French a gradual improvement of the living and construction standards of *lilong* was apparent. This proceeded from east to west, with single-family garden residences of the highest quality located in the western ends of the concessions. These divisions of housing quality according to social stratum persist today, and continues to reinforce the relationship between economics and location in the minds of Shanghai residents.

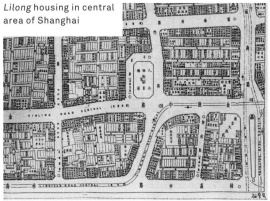

Lilong housing in central area of Shanghai

Single-family garden residence

A bird's-eye view of Shanghai taken in the 1920s

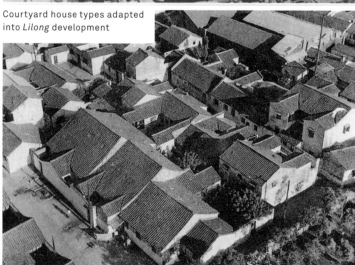

Courtyard house types adapted into *Lilong* development

Xiangning Li + Xiaochun Zhang

Four types of *Lilong* housing 1920s–30s

Hong De Li, One sample of the old style Shikumen *Lilong* housing

Garden *Lilong*

New style *Lilong*

Apartment *Lilong*

1949—84

From the founding of the People's Republic of China until the 1980s, land and housing were state-owned, and urban housing was provided as part of the planned economy through a welfare distribution system. Rents were collected, but the amount was negligible and its payment was largely symbolic.

In the 1950s, Shanghai began large-scale construction of neighborhoods for workers. In 1949, housing in the urban area of Shanghai totaled 23.59 million square meters, among which 15.63 million square meters were old-style *lilong* and slum houses. By 1960, the newly built workers housing projects in Shanghai totaled five million square meters, and shanties (self-built by local inhabitants) increased by 1.77 million square meters[1]. During this period, housing was poorly equipped to meet even minimum living standards: in most cases, several households would share a kitchen and one bathroom, as the apartments were connected by a corridor. Buildings averaged two to three floors.

The Cultural Revolution brought housing construction to a standstill in spite of the continued growth in population, effectively limiting the per capita living area of city residents at four square meters or less. In order to alleviate the pressure of such housing demand on a limited amount of land, Shanghai began to experiment with high-rise construction in the 1970s. These new buildings were generally twelve to sixteen stories tall, with a single corridor that faced north running along on each floor, and the provision of an individual kitchen and bathroom for each household.

During this period, housing was distributed by the government according to the number of family members in a household and the length of service of adult family members. Few had the right or ability to improve their quality of life. Defined by monotonous interior and exterior layouts, households differed from each other only in terms of square meters. Although social equality was maintained (in part due to the relatively small discrepancies in social standing) and newly built housing was indeed made available, living standards remained low in Shanghai. Existing *lilong* housing was also redistributed, with one unit oftentimes being shared by up to a dozen households, while single-family garden residences were only available to high-ranking government officials or other members of the politically powerful elite.

1 — See Li Zhenyu, *City•Housing•City* (Nanjing: Southeast University Press, 2004), p.42.

Xiangning Li + Xiaochun Zhang

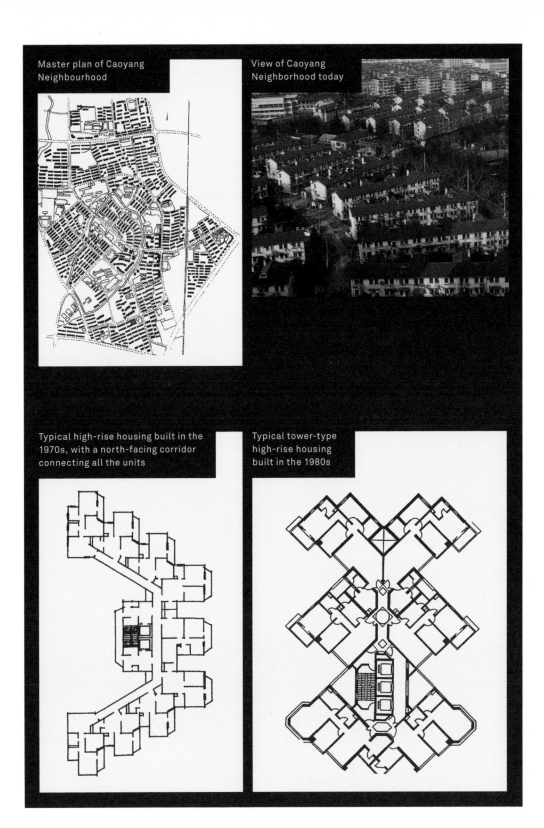

Master plan of Caoyang
Neighbourhood

View of Caoyang
Neighborhood today

Typical high-rise housing built in the
1970s, with a north-facing corridor
connecting all the units

Typical tower-type
high-rise housing
built in the 1980s

1984—Present

When the central Chinese government promulgated reform policy for urban housing supply and distribution in 1984, real estate interests began to play a critical role in housing supply and typology. This transitioned helped to usher in the commercialization of urban housing in the 1990s.

Since the latter half of the 1980s, Shanghai has mainly constructed high-rise towers, typically featuring multiple units surrounding one service core that combine elevators and staircases. Different from those built with north-facing corridors during the 1970s, these high-rises—varying between fifteen and thirty-three floors—emphasized natural lighting and ventilation, and provided less interference between households. Gradually, this became one of the major models for new housing construction in Shanghai[2]. With liberalization and market reforms, differences began to emerge in residents' incomes. Meanwhile, in then-newly developed areas of the city such as the Gubei district, commercial housing projects were built to target foreign customers. Housing design in Shanghai began to turn away from traditional and fixed models, paying greater heed to comfort and luxury living standards. But freedom to choose housing brought with it the differentiation, segregation and reconfiguration of urban space.

Since 1990, Shanghai has become a playground for domestic and foreign investors. Over USD 25 billion in international capital has been injected into the city's manufacturing industry. Many multinational companies have established regional headquarters in Shanghai, and nearly 100,000 foreigners have relocated to the city. Most of these expatriates belong to the high-income class, and, together with the Chinese *nouveau-riche*, they constitute an important demographic for the middle- and high-end commercial residences built since the 1990s. The so-called "international community" (usually referring to a neighborhood in which 30 percent of the population are foreigners) is a synonym for high-end lifestyles in contemporary Shanghai.

Xintiandi then (left) and now (right)

2 — Today, most new housing projects developed in Shanghai are high-rise towers (sometimes combined with mid-rise housing), and the most favorable floor plan is two-household units sharing one service elevator core. Most Shanghai residents believe that this model ensures the best natural light, ventilation and view.

Xiangning Li + Xiaochun Zhang

Yet, geographic associations from the past persist. Areas such as the historical French Concession and Xujiahui, where Western buildings have existed since before the revolution, remain prime locations today. Former industrial zones such as the Yangpu district still conjure poor environmental and living qualities. Foreigners, transplants from Hong Kong and Taiwan, and people with high-incomes usually opt for downtown, newly built and luxurious neighborhoods in Pudong or villas on the outskirts of the city. Those with mid- to high- incomes typically purchase apartments conveniently located along the city's major traffic arteries. Lower-middle-class households tend to live in housing obtained through the welfare distribution program, while low-income households are concentrated in *lilongs* within the old districts of the city. Unable to participate in the formal housing economy, Chinese rural migrants are pushed to unregulated shanties at the outskirts of the city.

With money in mind, contemporary Shanghai is beginning to recognize the value of its history and natural landscapes. Two residential projects exemplify this in particular. Thanks to recent investments to remediate Shanghai's waterfronts, housing along the Huangpu River and Suzhou Creek have become the site of luxury developments. Adaptive reuse is also underway in areas such as Taiping Bridge, where *lilongs* have been converted into bars and restaurants. These developments have brought skyrocketing rents with them.

Shanghai cannot continue to ignore the conflicts that emerge from razing the populist housing to make way for the rich. We await a new model: one that perpetuates social integration along with the city's legendary accumulation of material wealth.

Shimao Riviera Garden Neighborhood faces Huang Pu river and is one of the most expensive housing projects in Shanghai.

In the 1970s, Shanghai's *long-tangs* provided a village-like life in an urban setting. A rich tapestry of improvised street games brewed and bonded one generation of boys. A unique place and time, it was a short-lived world

Boys of "Long-Tang"
Weigang Qiu

Human habitats help to build or weaken social bonds, especially during one's childhood. Huifei, Liaoyuan, and I grew up together in a *long-tang*—an interconnected alley formed between rows of attached townhouses, with openings onto neighborhood shopping streets—in northern Shanghai in the 1970s. Shielded and hidden from the outside traffic, *long-tang*'s provided a safe, quiet, almost village-like life in the midst of a densely populated city. We were free to roam in the neighborhood passages and gathered there almost everyday for playtime. It helped that there were few manufactured toys available, not to mention television, Internet, or electronic games. That was the period when—before the implementation of the *One-Child* policy in the 1980s, and as a defense strategy against the Soviets and the US—large families were encouraged by Chairman Mao. Under a Stalinist economy and ideology, both of my parents worked full time. They never seemed to be bothered about supervising kids for safety, staying clean, or doing homework, arriving at our gathering places only when it was time for supper.

Kids are naturally inventive, and it helped that there were few manufactured toys available, and no TV, Internet, or electronic games. In the *long-tangs*, we collected bus tickets, cigarette and candy wrappers and bottle caps, repurposing each into a game. Waste paper from used newspaper and schoolbooks was amassed and folded into *si-guo-pian*—square-shaped pieces of origami to be exchanged in a game knocking each other's pieces out of a chalk-drawn square. Iron rings from discarded bicycle wheels and broken barrels were too tempting a toy to be thrown away: kids used bamboo and iron sticks to drive those rusty wheels around the neighborhood streets in droves, competing for how long the wheel could roll. Colorful glass marbles were a rare manufactured toy, and boys competed to win them in a precision game similar to miniature golf. Whenever a sand pile was dumped from a construction truck, it quickly became an anthill of crawling kids. We dug elaborately connected sand tunnels, set traps, and—inspired by World War II movies depicting Communist guerrilla fighters digging underground to ambush imperial Japanese invaders—pretended to be soldiers.

During long summer vacations, we took afternoon hikes out of our *long-tang* to public swimming pools, parks, and the city center. Modern-day parents would be horrified to hear that we traveled along railway tracks, frequently pressing an ear on the rails to listen for oncoming freight trains. Summer nights were the highlight of *long-tang* life, when the hot, humid Shanghai weather drove everyone out to the streets. Families set dinner tables outside and ate, adults chatted among themselves, kids played card and chess nearby, and in the process, unintentionally learned intimate family details of their neighbors. When the night fell, older kids played pranks on younger ones by telling ghost stories. During the August 2003 blackout in New York City, when I had to walk eight kilometers from Manhattan to my home in Queens, I was moved to see the sidewalks suddenly enlivened and filled with neighbors chatting with each other. It brought back childhood memories of Shanghai summer nights.

Remembering these childhood stories and moments, I can't help feeling sorry for kids growing up today in apartments or suburban homes in New York and Shanghai. Thanks to the rapid economic growth and construction boom in the last twenty years in China, my *long-tang* friends now all live in spacious, lavishly furnished apartments in newly constructed high-rises, and their children each have individual rooms. However, lifeless quietude seems to be the newest development in Shanghai today. Kids spend the summer taking English and piano lessons, playing video games on computers alone in their rooms, or connecting with friends in cyberspace. Nowadays, only grandparents or families of migrant workers are to be found in the remnants of *long-tang*'s, as young couples build their nests in new high-rises on the outskirts of the city instead.

Originally developed in the 1920s and 1930s, *long-tang*'s are significant form more than their morphology. The *long-tang* culture of the 1970s was a product of both a distinct human habitat and a specific period of China's political, social, and demographic histories. It disappeared as quickly as it arose, as perhaps deservedly so: Shanghai's *long-tang*'s were crowded, lacking in basic plumbing, and conflicts among neighbors were common. Yet, I am heartened to learn that leading architects in the world are now taking great interest in them and the ways of life they nurtured. With human ingenuity, innovative habitat designs that acknowledge and respect our instinct for close-knit, stable societies without sacrificing our need for safety, health, and comfort may emerge. I hope that one day the *long-tang*'s enjoy a rebirth for the next generation of kids in Shanghai.

Towards a Precipitous Typology
Silas Chiow

In nearly two decades, many of the residents of Beijing have moved from traditional brick courtyard houses, or hutongs, to gleaming high-rise apartment blocks. In Shanghai, inhabitants have similarly forgone shikumen or lane houses for new modern dwellings. China's rapid economic rise, led by government regulatory policies and fast-forward urbanization, have no doubt contributed to the growing trend of large-scale, mixed-use residential sub-centers that currently dot the Chinese landscape— a condition that offers a poignant contrast to the more conservative development models of most European, American and East Asian countries.

As an American architect whoc has been involved in Chinese projects for over thirteen years, and as someone who now calls Shanghai his home, I find this evolution of development typologies one of the most amazing aspects of contemporary Chinese urbanism. When I arrived in Shanghai in the early 1990s, much of what I discovered seemed frozen in the mid-twentieth century. But soon a number of government, market and social drivers precipitated a major shift from traditional low-rise housing to the construction of compact, mixed-use high-rises in dense urban areas. To be sure, a return to Shanghai as the century turned found a city almost unrecognizable, developing at a pace that seemed slowed by nothing in its path.

The Chinese government began leasing land in the early 1990s, with length of leases determined by the intended land use. While residential developments were allowed leases of up to 70 years, commercial and hotel developments were offered periods of only 40 or 60 years, respectively. Revenue was also divided into three streams: one-third devoted to the building of replacement housing for displaced families and individuals; another third set aside for upgrades to various regions' infrastructure and public structures, and a final third reserved for the creation of future public works. A decision by the State Council in 1994, intended to "deepen the reform of the urban housing system," further set three price points for home sales in terms of market, cost and standard.

Such major policy changes stood in sharp contrast to China's traditional welfare system, which had always provided housing to its citizens at relatively little cost. For instance, the Anju Project, aimed at solving the housing problems faced by medium- to low-income families within five years (1995-2000), was one program undertaken to add some 150 million square meters of low-rent living space to the nation's cities. But in July of 1998, China announced plans for a nationwide halt to the distribution of these homes, allowing them to enter the market at various prices through unregulated channels. Government-sponsored funding and discounts were also extended to those who purchased homes at market value, which spurred State-owned banks like the People's Bank of China and China Construction Bank to offer twenty-year mortgage loans to buyers for the first time in history.

This general relaxation of lending policies and other State-fueled financial incentives meanwhile led the Chinese economy to grow at rates on average of nine percent yearly. Coupled with the increasing demand for alternative investment vehicles by China's middle and upper classes, urban real estate markets continued to spike as city dwellers increasingly viewed new housing developments as opportunities to build personal wealth. In fact, over a half a million millionaires emerged from rising city centers during this time, no doubt inspired by the massive shift in real estate structures. On the other side of the coin, developers' appetite for density was fueled by friendly tax policies, as well as the huge demand for housing brought by an exodus from rural to urban areas. In order to satisfy these needs, high-rise buildings became the standard building typology.

Now it is common for most contemporary high-rises to designate lower space for retail outlets and service boutiques, as well as upper balconies and ad-on exterior spaces for anything from outdoor clothes drying to the storage of accumulated material goods. Furthermore, many middle-class families employ live-in maids, which require many new apartments to include a separate room and bath for their use. Such newfound desires for increased personal space belies the fact that Shanghai residents have been accustomed to five square meters of per capita living space for decades. Larger more luxurious units, however, have increased this space to that enjoyed by residents of London or Manhattan. Not surprisingly, in May 2007 the government announced plans to ensure that 70 percent of all residential development projects be dedicated to units of 90 square meters or less in order to increase supply of small- and medium-size housing.

At the time of the State Council's issue little over a decade ago, there were fewer than 100 high-rises in Shanghai. Nearly 1,000 exist today, and many other Chinese cities remain in the midst of their own building booms. Between 2001 and 2005, close to 1.3 billion square meters of new housing was built year on year: 570 million square meters in urban areas, and another 730 million in rural regions. Likewise, as ownership of China's lands has always lain with the central government, new regulations allowed it to simply seize existing properties to make way for more lucrative large-scale developments in prime urban locations.

Yet this phenomenon is relatively unique to China. The expropriation of property and clearing of large swaths of green space to make way for the 2008 Beijing Olympics, for which 1.5 million people were displaced with little or no compensation, is testament to China's development frenzy. By contrast, the 11.6 hectare Roppongi Hills project in Tokyo underwent more than two decades of negotiations while the developer secured land-use permission from each of the 800 families living on it at the time. Limited regulation at the federal level generally results in a slower evolution of building typologies in say, Chicago or New York, where urbanization trends and real estate markets have had more time to mature.

Silas Chiow

In 2006, China finally tightened lending to developers and heightened its supervision over land use to cool overheated real estate markets. Still, property investment continued to grow 27.4 percent to USD 68.6 billion by May of 2007 over the prior year, with total investment in China's skyrocketing real estate sector reaching an estimated USD 657.6 billion, according to the Chinese Ministry of Construction. Recently promised easy financing and swift, high returns on their investments, aggressive developers continue to acquire large parcels of land, especially in China's less-developed central and western regions. As a result, a number of poorly conceived large-scale development projects continue to proliferate, slapped together with little regard for users or the environment in pursuit of quick turnover times.

The market remains saturated with such project types: mixed-used high-rises that integrate a variety of residential, commercial and retail services to accommodate the myriad needs of urban residents. Today, the disposable income of a Shanghainese is nearly double that of the average citizen, many nestled in sprawling island oases that look after the safety and welfare of their own, far removed from important civic structures and engagement. Middle-income families desire bigger cars and homes in close proximity to workplaces and the intimacy of a tight-knit (albeit surrogate) community. Propelled by the weight of its own momentum, this overall commodification of lifestyles in the 21st century Chinese city presents deeper challenges as the growing gap between China's rich and poor expands, and a rapid transformation of typologies struggles to sustain an entirely new way of living.

Environmental Transformation

Green Space Use
2020

Woods & Landscaped Open Space
Waterfront Greenery
Greenbelt
Roadside Greenery
Public Greenery

Yangtze River

Huangpu River

Sheshan National
Resort Zone

Dongwangsha Natural
Reservation Zone

Hangzhou Bay

Da-Xiao Jinshan
Natural Reservation Zone

N

0 1   5   10   20 km

Sources: *Summary of the Comprehensive Plan of Shanghai (1999-2020).* Shanghai Urban Planning
Administration Bureau. Shanghai Urban Planning and Design Research Institute.
Shanghai Statistical Yearbook 2006. Shanghai Municipal Statistics Bureau.
(Beijing: China Statistics Press, 2006) Table 11.15

Green Space
1980–2005

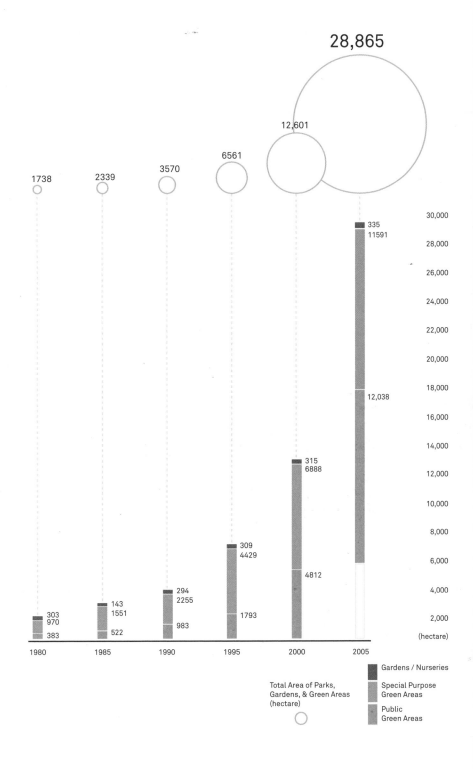

28,865

12,601

6561

1738   2339   3570

	30,000
	28,000
	26,000
	24,000
	22,000
	20,000
	18,000
	16,000
	14,000
	12,000
	10,000
	8,000
	6,000
	4,000
	2,000
	(hectare)

335
11591

12,038

315
6888

4812

309
4429

1793

294
2255

143
1551

983

303
970

383   522

1980   1985   1990   1995   2000   2005

Total Area of Parks,
Gardens, & Green Areas
(hectare)

Gardens / Nurseries

Special Purpose
Green Areas

Public
Green Areas

Sensitive Ecological Areas
2020

■ Sensitive Ecological Area

Yangtze River

Huangpu River

Hangzhou Bay

N

Sources: *Summary of the Comprehensive Plan of Shanghai (1999-2020)*. Shanghai Urban Planning
Administration Bureau. Shanghai Urban Planning and Design Research Institute.
Shanghai Statistical Yearbook 2006. Shanghai Municipal Statistics Bureau.
(Beijing: China Statistics Press, 2006) Table 11.15, 11.16, 12.12.

0 1   5   10   20 km

Trees and Forestry

1980-2005

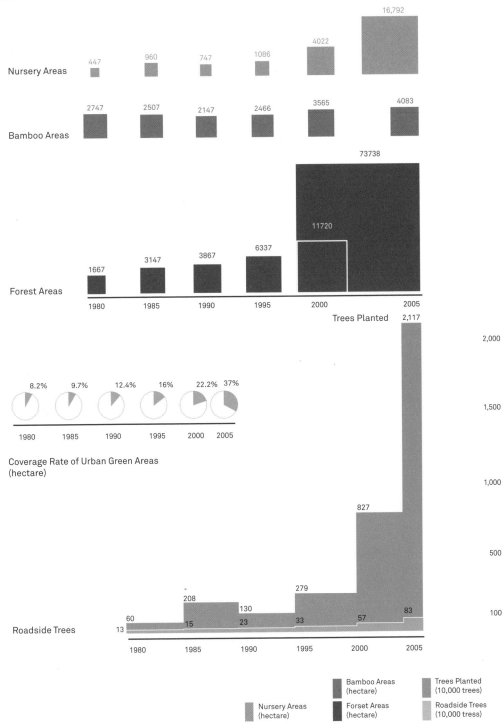

Nursery Areas

447 960 747 1086 4022 16,792

Bamboo Areas

2747 2507 2147 2466 3565 4083

Forest Areas

1667 3147 3867 6337 11720 73738

1980 1985 1990 1995 2000 2005

Trees Planted
2,117

Coverage Rate of Urban Green Areas
(hectare)

8.2% 9.7% 12.4% 16% 22.2% 37%

1980 1985 1990 1995 2000 2005

2,000

1,500

1,000

827

500

279

208
130

60
13 15 23 33 57 83 100

Roadside Trees

1980 1985 1990 1995 2000 2005

Nursery Areas
(hectare)

Bamboo Areas
(hectare)

Forset Areas
(hectare)

Trees Planted
(10,000 trees)

Roadside Trees
(10,000 tress)

Tap Water
1990-2005

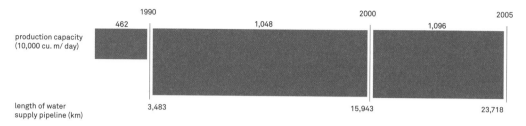

production capacity (10,000 cu. m/ day)

1990	2000	2005
462	1,048	1,096

length of water supply pipeline (km)

3,483   15,943   23,718

daily average water consumed

335,600 litres   541,200 litres   624,800 litres

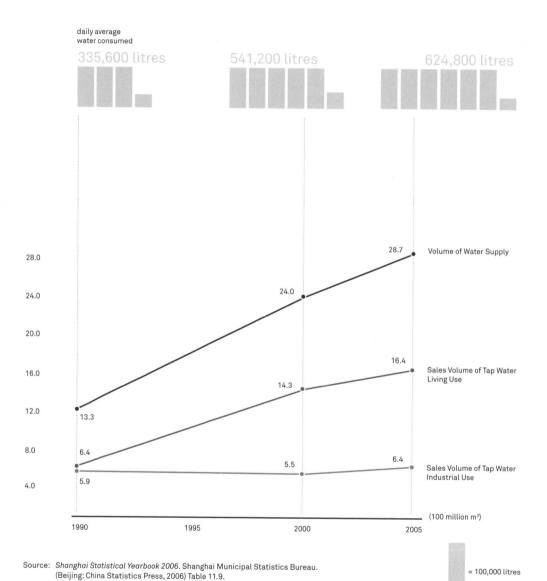

Volume of Water Supply

28.7
24.0
13.3

Sales Volume of Tap Water Living Use

16.4
14.3
6.4

Sales Volume of Tap Water Industrial Use

5.9
5.5
6.4

(100 million m³)

28.0
24.0
20.0
16.0
12.0
8.0
4.0

1990   1995   2000   2005

= 100,000 litres

Source: *Shanghai Statistical Yearbook 2006*. Shanghai Municipal Statistics Bureau. (Beijing: China Statistics Press, 2006) Table 11.9.

Water Protection

1991-2005

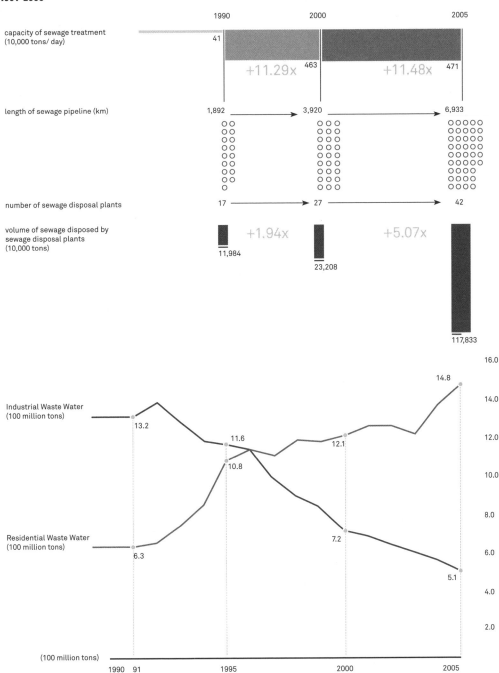

capacity of sewage treatment (10,000 tons/ day)

1990   2000   2005

41

+11.29x   463   +11.48x   471

length of sewage pipeline (km)

1,892 → 3,920 → 6,933

number of sewage disposal plants

17 → 27 → 42

volume of sewage disposed by sewage disposal plants (10,000 tons)

+1.94x   +5.07x

11,984

23,208

117,833

Industrial Waste Water (100 million tons)

13.2   11.6   12.1   14.8

10.8

Residential Waste Water (100 million tons)

6.3   7.2   5.1

16.0
14.0
12.0
10.0
8.0
6.0
4.0
2.0

(100 million tons)

1990 91   1995   2000   2005

Source: *Shanghai Statistical Yearbook 2006*. Shanghai Municipal Statistics Bureau.
(Beijing: China Statistics Press, 2006) Table 20.3.

Yangtze River

The Yangtze River Basin, 1,800,000 km^2, is the home to 420 million people or 1/3 the entire population of China.
The shipping capacity on the mainstream of the Yangtze reached 975 million tons in 2005 and will grow to 1.3 billion tons by the year 2010.

Source: UNITAR Hiroshima Office for Asia and the Pacific, Series on Biodiversity.
Training Workshop on Wetlands, Biodiversity and Water: New Tools for the Ecosystem Management. Kushiro, Japan, 29 November to 3 December 2004. Kushiro International Wetland Centre.

Huangpu River

Huangpu River Central Area covers an area of 29.3 km² from Xiangyin Road Tunnel in the north to Lupu Bridge in the South.
The northern extension starts from Wusong Estuary in the north to Xiangyin Road Tunnel in the south, covering 27.3 km² in the plan.
The southern extension stretches from Lupu Bridge down to Xupu Bridge with a planning area of 16.7 km².

Source: Shanghai Urban Planning Exhibition Center.

Suzhou Creek (Wusang River)

Originates from Guajingkou of Taihu Lake. Suzhou Creek is 125 km long in total, of which 53.1 km is within Shanghai Municipality. Enter Shanghai Municipality at Qingpu District, traverse nine administrative districts, connects with Huangpu River at Waibaidu Bridge.

Suzhou Creek Rehabilitation. Phase I
Implementing from 1998 to 2002 with a total investment of 6.998 billion yuan RMB Rehabilitation core: planning overall, combining short-term and long-term horizons, stressing focal points, and implementing step by step.

Phase II
Investing from 2003 to 2005 with a total investment of 3.77 billion yuan RMB Rehabilitation core: emphasis on rehabilitating water whilst laying stress on eradication and promoting the riverside development.

Source: Shanghai Urban Planning Exhibition Center

Energy Consumption

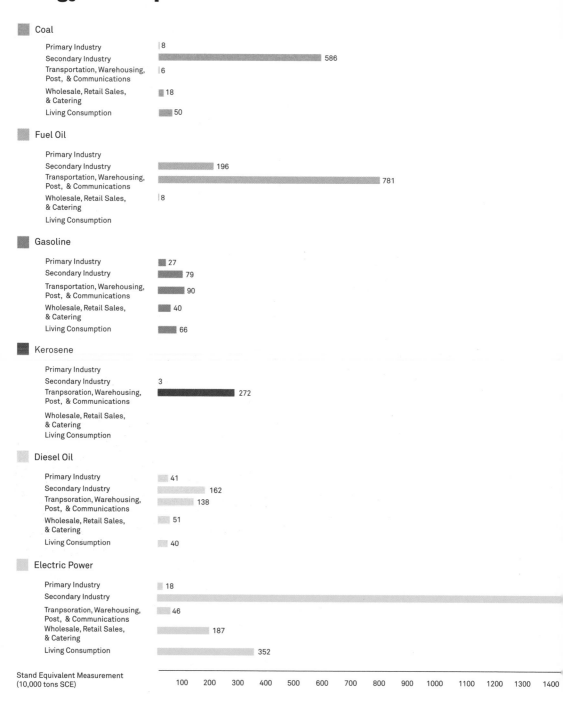

Coal

Primary Industry	8
Secondary Industry	586
Transportation, Warehousing, Post, & Communications	6
Wholesale, Retail Sales, & Catering	18
Living Consumption	50

Fuel Oil

Primary Industry	
Secondary Industry	196
Transportation, Warehousing, Post, & Communications	781
Wholesale, Retail Sales, & Catering	8
Living Consumption	

Gasoline

Primary Industry	27
Secondary Industry	79
Transportation, Warehousing, Post, & Communications	90
Wholesale, Retail Sales, & Catering	40
Living Consumption	66

Kerosene

Primary Industry	
Secondary Industry	3
Transpsoration, Warehousing, Post, & Communications	272
Wholesale, Retail Sales, & Catering	
Living Consumption	

Diesel Oil

Primary Industry	41
Secondary Industry	162
Transpsoration, Warehousing, Post, & Communications	138
Wholesale, Retail Sales, & Catering	51
Living Consumption	40

Electric Power

Primary Industry	18
Secondary Industry	
Transpsoration, Warehousing, Post, & Communications	46
Wholesale, Retail Sales, & Catering	187
Living Consumption	352

Stand Equivalent Measurement (10,000 tons SCE)

100 200 300 400 500 600 700 800 900 1000 1100 1200 1300 1400

Source: *Shanghai Statistical Yearbook 2006*. Shanghai Municipal Statistics Bureau.
(Beijing: China Statistics Press, 2006) Table 6.3, 6.4, 6.6, 6.9.

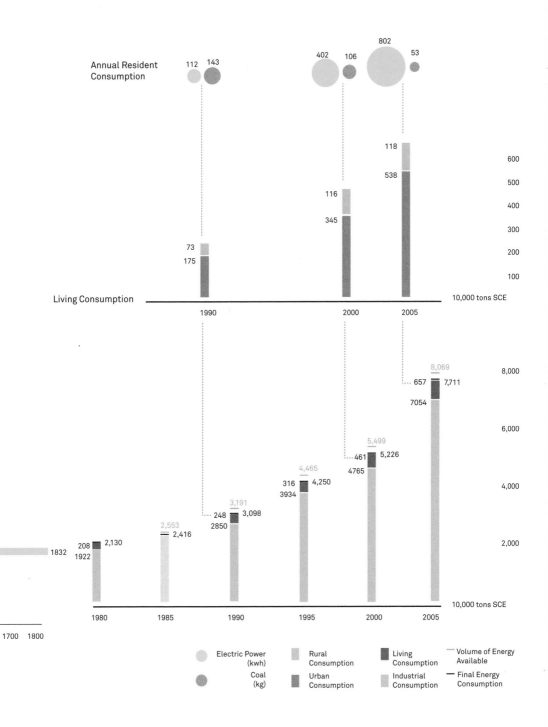

Annual Resident Consumption

Living Consumption   10,000 tons SCE

Air Pollution
2000-2005

Annual Daily Mean Concentration
of SO_2 in Urban Area
(mg/ m^3)

.061

.045

Annual Daily Mean Concentration
of NO_2 in Urban Area
(mg/ m^3)

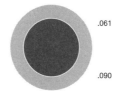

.061

.090

Mean Concentration of Inhalable
Particulate in Urban Area
(mg/ m^3)

.088

Frequency of Acid Rain

26%   40%

2000   2005

Number of Days with Good Ambient
Air Quality (day)

2000   2005

295   322

2000   2005

Source: *Shanghai Statistical Yearbook 2006*. Shanghai Municipal Statistics Bureau.
          (Beijing: China Statistics Press, 2006) Table 20.4, 20.5.

Total Emission

1991–2005

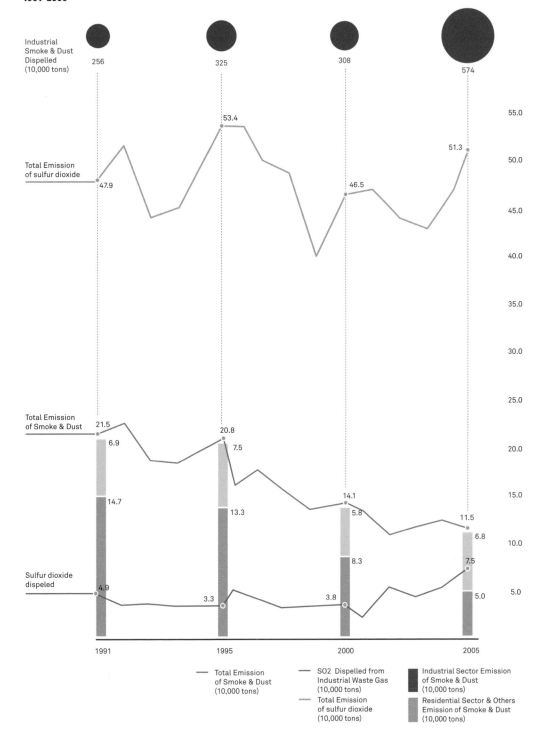

Industrial Smoke & Dust Dispelled (10,000 tons)

256   325   308   574

Total Emission of sulfur dioxide

55.0

53.4   51.3

47.9   46.5

50.0

45.0

40.0

35.0

30.0

25.0

Total Emission of Smoke & Dust

21.5   6.9   20.8   7.5   14.1   5.8   11.5   6.8

20.0

14.7   13.3   8.3   7.5

15.0

Sulfur dioxide dispeled

4.9   3.3   3.8   5.0

10.0

5.0

1991   1995   2000   2005

—— Total Emission of Smoke & Dust (10,000 tons)

—— SO2 Dispelled from Industrial Waste Gas (10,000 tons)

■ Industrial Sector Emission of Smoke & Dust (10,000 tons)

—— Total Emission of sulfur dioxide (10,000 tons)

■ Residential Sector & Others Emission of Smoke & Dust (10,000 tons)

Urban Sanitation

1980–2005

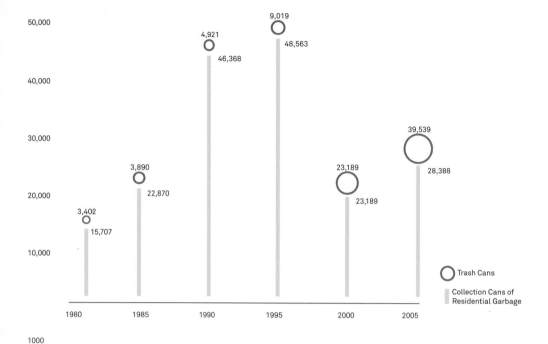

50,000
40,000
30,000
20,000
10,000

3,402
15,707
1980

3,890
22,870
1985

4,921
46,368
1990

9,019
48,563
1995

23,189
23,189
2000

39,539
28,388
2005

○ Trash Cans

▌ Collection Cans of
Residential Garbage

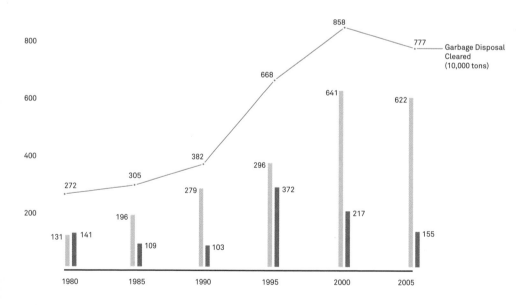

1000

800

600

400

200

272
131 141
1980

305
196 109
1985

382
279 103
1990

296 372
1995

858
641 217
2000

777
622 155
2005

668

Garbage Disposal
Cleared
(10,000 tons)

▌ Residential
Garbage

▌ Construction
Garbage

Source: *Shanghai Statistical Yearbook 2006*. Shanghai Municipal Statistics Bureau.
(Beijing: China Statistics Press, 2006) Table 20.7

Sinking City
1921-2007

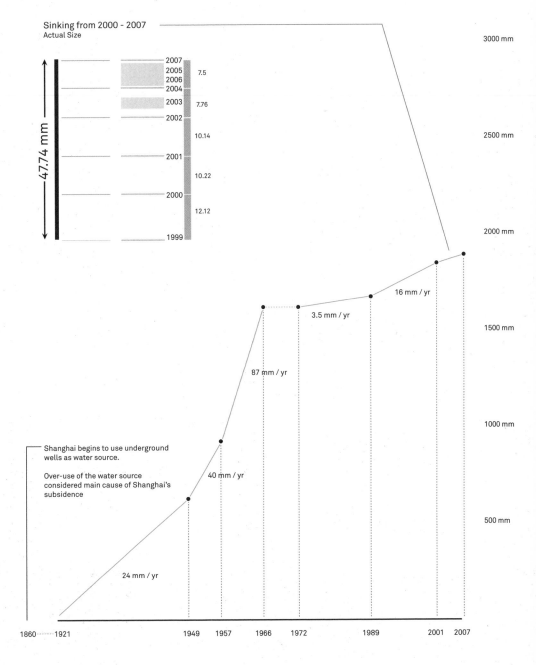

Sinking from 2000 - 2007
Actual Size

47.74 mm

2007	
2005	7.5
2006	
2004	
2003	7.76
2002	
	10.14
2001	
	10.22
2000	
	12.12
1999	

3000 mm

2500 mm

2000 mm

16 mm / yr

1500 mm

3.5 mm / yr

87 mm / yr

1000 mm

Shanghai begins to use underground wells as water source.

Over-use of the water source considered main cause of Shanghai's subsidence

40 mm / yr

500 mm

24 mm / yr

1860 ····· 1921   1949 1957 1966 1972   1989   2001 2007

Sources: http://www.chinadaily.com.cn/en/doc/2003-11/19/content_282844.htm
China Daily, "Shanghai Still Sinking," China Daily, chinadaily.com.cn, November 11, 2003. (accessed October 30, 2007).
http://www.chinadaily.com.cn/en/doc/2003-07/16/content_245660.htm
China Daily, "Shanghai puts up a fight to stop sinking," China Daily, chinadaily.com.cn, July 16, 2007. (accessed October 30, 2007).
http://www.10thnpc.org.cn/english/environment/220032.htm
China Daily Hong Kong Edition, "Shanghai Sinking 5-7mm Annually," CHINA.ORG.CN, August 7, 2007 (accessed October 30, 2007).
http://english.china.org.cn/english/2002/Sep/42481.htm
China Daily, "Shanghai Tries to Prevent Ground Sinking" CHINA.ORG.CN, September 10, 2002. (accessed October 30, 2007).

百货
RTMENT ST

商店

ORE

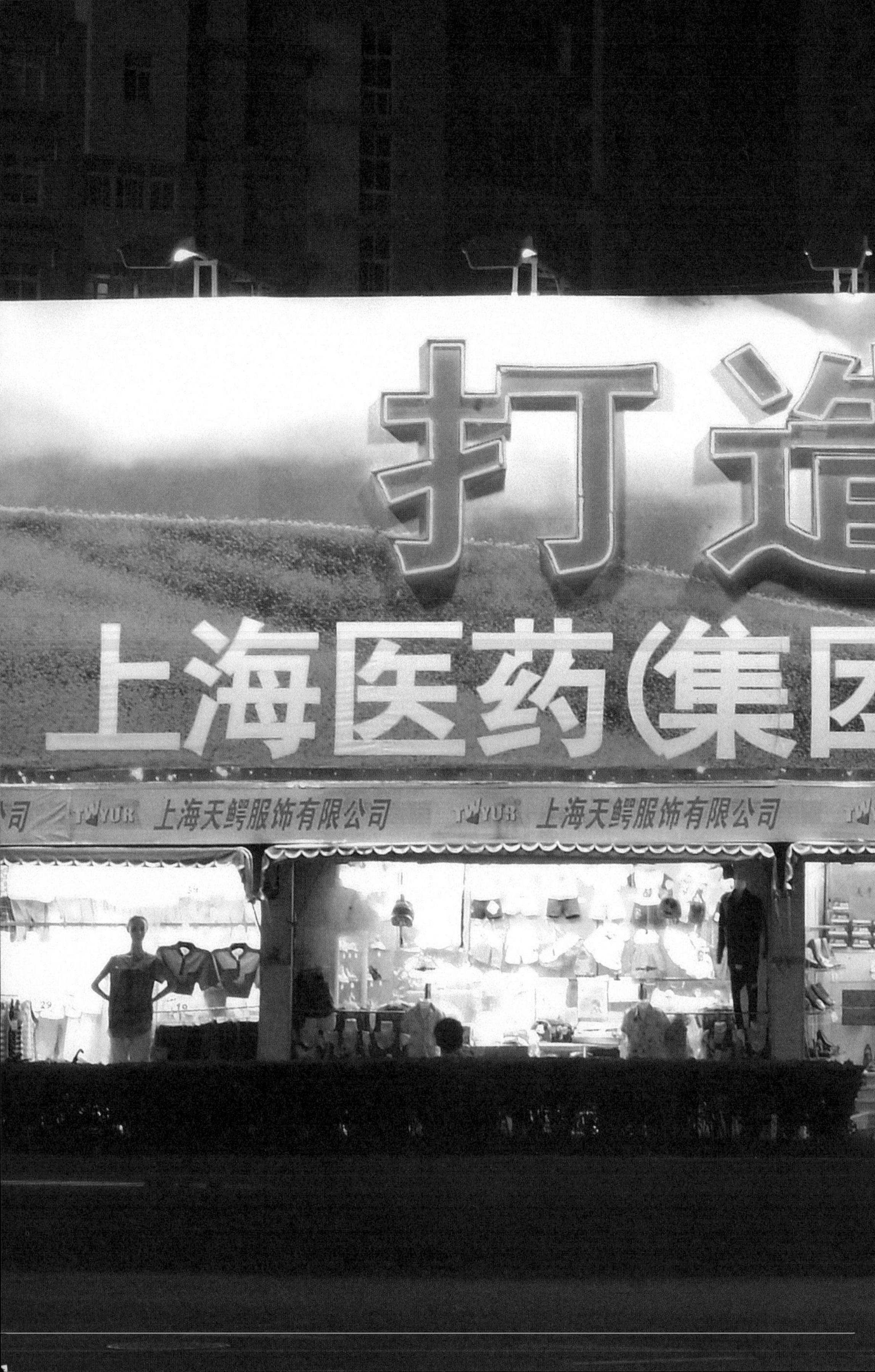

Poles
Sol Madridejos
Juan Carlos Sancho

I. The City

Urban-scale projects require an unstable but nonetheless clear and pragmatic action strategy if we are to tackle the city's social, cultural, economic and environmental complexity. It is essential to carry out a clear diagnosis and establish action mechanisms— and not only passive ways of looking and analyzing—that will also allow for "on-site" decisions, affecting the design process "on the fly." These actions do not define new urban variables, but rather concentrate, connect or activate existing ones into a new unitary and networked system, generating points, lines, networks, and tension fields that are materialized in what we call "poles."

Within this system (referred to here as the city) the structure that is generated arises from the confrontation of a double scale—urban and architectural—and a strategic convergence and interaction between the two. This is closer to what is usually called the master plan; something that is appropriate to the particular features of each project, each place and each situation, a flexible, changing strategy that responds to each environment and each moment.

In the urban projects that we have designed and developed over the last few years, this strategy has been affected by the scale, history, culture and the social requirements of the brief as well as by the economic forces of each situation and place. Each project is presented with a series of non-stable variables in which the memory of the past (historic-cultural) is diluted by future requirements, with uncertainty and a need for adaptation as predominant conditions. The design process is shaped by the perception, analysis and diagnosis of which forces have to be activated in each project.

II. Poles

Poles define the initial activation of each project and are manifested in different ways according to each situation. Poles can be:

— **Points of reference** concentrating symbolic, social and cultural activity at an urban scale. In the project for the edges of the HuangPu River in Shanghai, we propose different city models that take into account a series of urban variables—typology, scale, urban structure (*lilongs*), function—and that are activated by the contrasting position of certain symbolic and perceptive points of reference.

— **Bars**, a strategy (both urban and spatial) of constant adaptation to the tensions that exist in the city. We use bars as an adaptive response to the relationship, direction and involvement within these tensions. Bars contain continuous space with variable sections and they can bend, rise and cross over each other in response to outside influences. In the Doulum Art Forum (Shanghai) these spatial models adapt to the different site conditions.

— **Centers** that convene, attract and generate social activity. In the urban project for the historic center of Chang-xing, activity centers enhance public occupation of the city and act as a complementary counterpoint to the traditional city center.

— **Stripes**. Bars combine to form a tapestry, an urban texture characterized by a rhythm of scales, functions, and edges. In the project for the new Qingpu residential district, the different residential and public conditions modify a mixed urban structure capable of relating to the surrounding environment.

The city arises from the overlap and interrelation between all its tensions, directions, connections, focal points, limits, bars, voids, textures, functions, qualities, scales, and densities (built-up, green, hard, spatial or occasional). This overlap and contrast of forces create the active networks that, as an urban musical score, provide the platform for diverse social rhythms.

Chongming Island:
Greening Shanghai
in the Twenty-First Century
Philip Enquist

As Shanghai grows in population and expands its urban footprint, the natural environment and agriculture of this region are increasingly impacted. The city's rapid sprawl from its historic Huangpu River center has affected the region with poor air quality, traffic congestion, and expansive development. While Shanghai struggles to meet the needs of its growing office, commercial, industrial and residential markets, the environment is getting left further and further behind.

As Shanghai—China's most energetic and forward thinking city—moves into the twenty-first century, it is critical that it commit to ecological best practices in city and regional design. Beyond its commercial muscle and dramatic architecture, Shanghai can become China's role model for green urban design: boasting clean air, significant public park and waterfront systems, a transport infrastructure and large-scale open space reserves.

One example of Shanghai's new, green thinking is demonstrated in the recent planning of Chongming Island, the largest alluvial island in the world (one-fifth of Shanghai's region). It sits just a few kilometers north of central Shanghai in the Yangtze River, and stretches 80 kilometers to the east, up river toward Suzhou.

In 2003, the City hosted a competition to generate ideas for how to position this island for future development. Traditionally a remote place—only accessible by boat—Chongming will be connected to Shanghai and the region by a major bridge and tunnel system traversing the Yangtze. It will soon be connected to the international airport as well.

Chongming Island has been created over centuries by the soil deposits from the Yangtze, and continues to grow today. It is 1,000 square kilometers of clean and fertile soils supporting an extensive wetland system and home to many birds and animals.

During the Cultural Revolution, many people were brought to Chongming to construct an extensive levee and canal system to protect the island from flooding, and to create an irrigation system for farming. Food production was—and still is—the main mission for this island. Rich soil and water made Chongming the food basket for Shanghai, producing fruits, vegetables, shrimp, crab, fish, and meat products.

Now that the highway connection is certain, developers are lining up to identify manufacturing sites, theme parks, housing and commercial developments. The current population of the island ranges from 500,000 to 600,000 people. Projected growth estimates a population boom to somewhere close to 2,000,000.

Skidmore, Owings and Merrill's (SOM's) urban design studio from Chicago proposed the winning strategy for the island. The proposed plan for a "green island" recognized that the strength and core business of the island is food. Farming should be respected and strengthened as the identifying industry of the island. In addition, the green and wet environment suggested a more sensitive approach to wetland restoration and preservation of the wilderness areas. Finally, tight clustering of compact, transit oriented communities and villages would minimize impact on the land.

The proposed development strategy consisted of eight principles that guided growth and future decision making for all uses. These included:

1. Wilderness and Ecosystems
2. Organic Farming
3. Green Systems and Infrastructure
4. Green Industries and Research
5. A Reliance on Transit
6. Ecotourism
7. Farming Villages
8. Compact Coastal Cities

In 2004, Chinese President Hu Jintao promoted the Chongming Island Plan as a national model for sustainability, energy efficiency and environmental awareness. It was a very clear message to the region, country and the world that China is entering a new age of continued prosperity through sustainable practices and environmental awareness.

Zhou Jian, Director of Tongi University's School of Architecture and Urban Planning in Shanghai, has also endorsed the plan, stating: "The reality is that China lacks land for farming and energy resources, and has a huge population on top of it all. It was inevitable that we would favor a sustainable design plan like SOM's."

One year into the plan, great accomplishments have been made by the Shanghai government. Planning is underway for one of the first cities on the eastern end, which explores low- and zero-energy aspirations in accordance with larger island aspirations. Parkway strategies are also being explored for an expanded roadway system that will eventually lead to the new bridge.

Philip Enquist

Eight Principles for Chongming Island

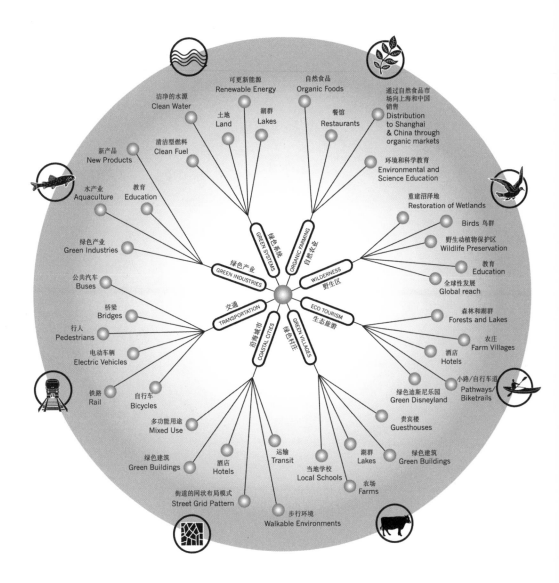

可更新能源 Renewable Energy
自然食品 Organic Foods
洁净的水源 Clean Water
土地 Land
潮群 Lakes
餐馆 Restaurants
通过自然食品市场向上海和中国销售 Distribution to Shanghai & China through organic markets
清洁型燃料 Clean Fuel
环境和科学教育 Environmental and Science Education
新产品 New Products
重建沼泽地 Restoration of Wetlands
水产业 Aquaculture
教育 Education
Birds 鸟群
野生动植物保护区 Wildlife Preservation
绿色产业 Green Industries
教育 Education
绿色系统 GREEN SYSTEMS
自然农业 ORGANIC FARMING
全球性发展 Global reach
绿色产业 GREEN INDUSTRIES
野生区 WILDERNESS
公共汽车 Buses
森林和潮群 Forests and Lakes
桥梁 Bridges
交通 TRANSPORTATION
生态旅游 ECO TOURISM
农庄 Farm Villages
行人 Pedestrians
酒店 Hotels
电动车辆 Electric Vehicles
沿海城市 COASTAL CITIES
绿色村庄 GREEN VILLAGES
小路/自行车道 Pathways/ Biketrails
铁路 Rail
自行车 Bicycles
绿色迪斯尼乐园 Green Disneyland
多功能用途 Mixed Use
贵宾楼 Guesthouses
绿色建筑 Green Buildings
酒店 Hotels
运输 Transit
当地学校 Local Schools
潮群 Lakes
绿色建筑 Green Buildings
街道的网状布局模式 Street Grid Pattern
农场 Farms
步行环境 Walkable Environments

The challenge is to transform a coastal rural island into a world class sustainable district for Shanghai
 that preserves the environment yet houses up to 2,000,000 people.

Philip Enquist

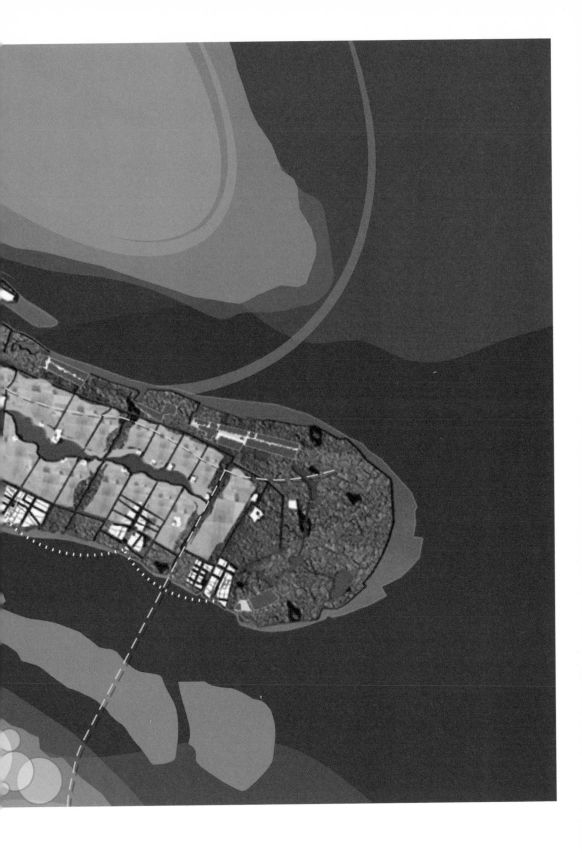

1. Wilderness and Ecosystems

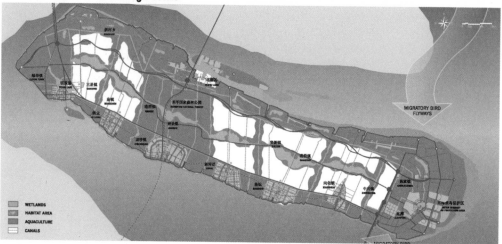

A preservation and restoration strategy for the island's extensive wetlands was proposed. Saving these areas will support the habitats for migratory birds, Chinese alligators, and numerous other life forms that live on the island. It also highlighted the interdependent relationship between the island and the Yangtze River. The wetlands are also seen as a focal point for scenic tourism and education for Shanghai residents.

2. Organic Farming

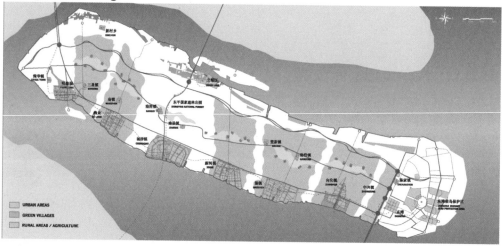

In order to bolster the island's agricultural identity while simultaneously increasing farmer's income and strengthening Shanghai's association with cuisine, farmers will be encouraged to go organic and align directly with local restaurants for the sale of food products. This alliance with the restaurant industry will produce an increase in farmers' yearly income. Restaurants, on the other hand, will see greater consistency and quality in their food products.

Philip Enquist

3. Green Systems and Infrastructure

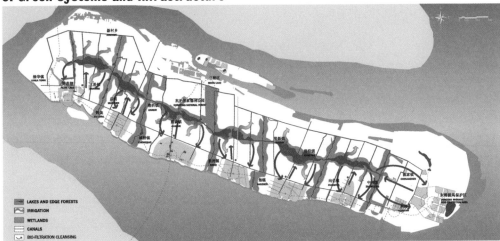

The use of wetlands, canals and a lake system to recycle grey water and address storm water was proposed. Continuous sea breezes suggested opportunities for harvesting wind energy to gradually replace coal burning power plants found on the island today. The lake system will also be used to create a hydrostatic pressure thereby keeping the salt water out of the ground water table.

4. Green Industries and Research

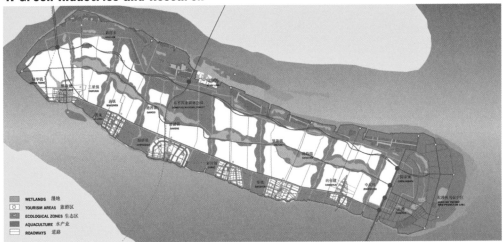

As new industries are attracted to Chongming Island, the government will emphasize new technologies related to sustainable industries, green building products, electric vehicle research, renewable energy technologies and biofuel research. Themes of green industries, product development and research were proposed. Local universities will be encouraged to partner with industries in this unique national mission.

5. A Reliance on Transit

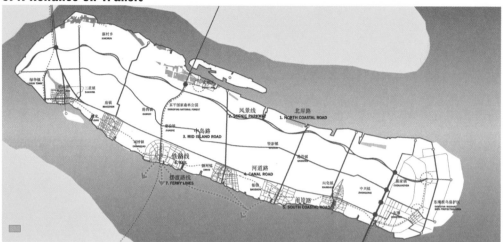

A rail system linking all major settlements on Chongming Island to Shanghai, alongside an electric bus system for local transport within and between cities and villages were proposed. Electric vehicles and electric scooters—all currently manufactured in China—were emphasized, as well as bicycles. Street designs will incorporate bicycle lanes, and walkability within each community will be encouraged.

6. Ecotourism

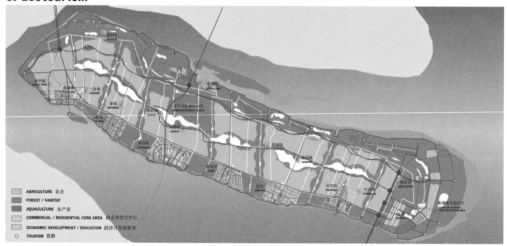

Located only one hour from Shanghai, Chongming Island lies within reasonable distance for taking a weekend in the country. Educational institutions, conference centers, hotels and resort destinations can all create the components of this new industry, and do so within the environmental mission of the island. The combined industry of agriculture, ecology and tourism was proposed as a viable economic engine for Shanghai residents with few places to go to find respite from the urban environment.

Philip Enquist

7. Farming Villages

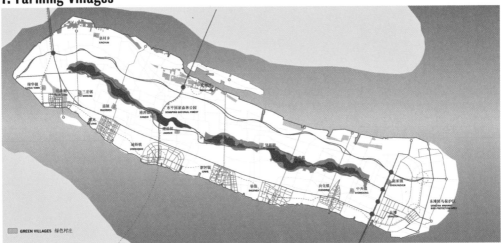

Many small farming villages dot the island. The village structure will be respected and protected, as they provide convenient access to farmlands and help to distribute the population into small neighborhood communities. Schools, neighborhood commercial, community services, together with some potential tourism facilities, restaurants, small inns, and health facilities can all integrate within a typical village.

8. Compact Coastal Cities

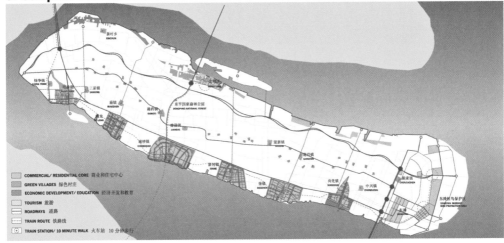

Eight sites for cities have been identified along Chongming's south coast. Some of these cities exist today and some are new. Cities will be an average of eight to sixteen kilometers apart. All will be harbor cities with direct boat access to Shanghai. Each city will support approximately 100,000 to 300,000 people and will have central rail access. Each community was proposed as mixed-use with residential, industry, commercial and educational facilities. Industries are intended to coexist with each community to encourage living and working in close proximity.

Contributors

Silas Chiow, AIA, serves as Director of China at Skidmore, Owings and Merrill (SOM) in Shanghai. He is responsible for spearheading SOM's business strategies, as well as directing the firm's architecture and planning projects throughout China and greater Asia. Over the last 21 years, Mr. Chiow has developed his expertise to include a variety of project types, from commercial and mixed-use developments to hotels, convention centers, and cultural institutions.

Andrew Clark is a designer at Bruce Mau Design in Chicago. He has participated in the exhibition and publication Dresser Trunk Project, the design and exhibition Envisioning the Bloomingdale Line, and Exchange, an installation for American Institute of Architects (AIA) Chicago. While studying architecture at the University of Illinois at Chicago, he collaborated at UIC's City Design Center, a multi-disciplinary research, education, and service institution, and participated in the Mayor's Institute on City Design. Andrew has most recently joined MAS Studio in Chicago, an architecture and urban design firm based in Chicago and Barcelona.

Philip Enquist is an architect and urban planner, who leads the Urban Design & Planning studio at Skidmore, Owings and Merrill LLP (SOM) in Chicago. He collaborates closely with government agencies and community groups to shape the places we live and work. He has directed planning and design on a variety of downtown mixed-use projects, new towns, campus master plans, as well as regional planning initiatives.

Greg Girard is a Canadian photographer who has spent much of his life in Asia. His latest book *Phantom Shanghai* (Magenta, 2007) documents the Shanghai that will not survive the vision the city has for itself. Other published work includes the book *City of Darkness* (Watermark, 1999), in collaboration with Ian Lambot, a record of the final years of Hong Kong's infamous Kowloon Walled City. He lives in Shanghai.

Iker Gil is an architect, urban designer, and director of MAS studio, a collaborative architecture and urban design firm with a multidisciplinary approach to a wide range of projects. MAS studio also develops its work in other fields such as research, exhibitions and publications. In addition, he teaches at the University of Illinois at Chicago, is a contributor at Arketypo Magazine and the delegate in the US for the "BIO Bienal Internacional de Arquitectura. Bilbao 2009". Iker also works in the Urban Design and Planning studio at SOM Chicago, where he has been a lead designer for projects in the US, Europe and China.

Sharon Haar is an architect and Associate Professor at the University of Illinois at Chicago (UIC) where she teaches housing design and urban design and theory. She has published several books and is working on a book titled *City As Campus: Sites of Urban Education*. She is currently the Book Review Editor for the Journal of Architectural Education.

Xiangning Li received his Ph.D. from Tongji University in 2004. He is currently a lecturer of Architectural History and Theory, and assistant dean of the Tongji University College of Architecture and Urban Planning. He has published widely on contemporary Chinese architecture and urbanism. He also serves as a guest editor of Time+Architecture.

Sol Madridejos is an architect and Professor at the European University of Madrid, CEES. Co-founded Sancho-Madridejos Architecture Office in 1997, which is currently developing several projects in China. Their work has been widely published and recently exhibited in On-Site: New Architecture in Spain in the MoMA.

Jonathan Miller is a Professor of film studies at the Illinois Institute of Technology (IIT) and visiting faculty at the University of Illinois at Chicago (UIC). He is a film critic for WBEZ, Chicago Public Radio. He has also been a writer for the Learning from North Lawndale exhibition (Chicago Architectural Foundation) and the curator of the exhibition Traps (Extension Gallery).

Juan de Dios Perez is a photographer and Professor in several photography schools in Barcelona. He has participated in numerous collective and individual exhibitions, including *Amateur, Abtauchen, Memorias Anonimas, Sombras*, and *Territorios del Instante*. He is a regular collaborator with publishers such as Santa & Cole and designers such as Mariona Garcia. His work has been published in several books and periodicals.

Weigang Qiu is an Assistant Professor of Evolutionary Informatics and Microbial Diversity at the Department of Biological Sciences at Hunter College, New York. Dr Qiu was born and grew up in Shanghai, getting his B. Sc. degree in Biochemistry from Fudan University, Shanghai (1986), and his Master's Degree in Biotechnology from the Shanghai Jiao Tong University.

Peter G. Rowe is the Raymond Garbe Professor of Architecture and Urban Design and University Distinguished Service Professor at the Graduate School of Design, Harvard University, where he has taught since 1985. He served as Dean of the Faculty of Design (1992-2004) and was Director of the School of Architecture at Rice University (1981-1985).

Juan Carlos Sancho is an architect and Professor at the Madrid School of Architecture (ETSAM) since 1990, and sub-director of projects department since 1998. Co-founded Sancho-Madridejos Architecture Office in 1997, which is currently developing several projects in China. Their work has been widely published and recently exhibited in On-Site: New Architecture in Spain in the MoMA.

Saskia Sassen is the Ralph Lewis Professor of Sociology at the University of Chicago and Centennial Visiting Professor at the London School of Economics. She has served as co-director of the Economy Section of the Global Chicago Project, a Member of the National Academy of Sciences Panel on Urban Data Sets, a Member of the Council of Foreign Relations, and Chair of the Information Technology, International Cooperation and Global Security Committee of the SSRC.

Denise Scott Brown is an architect, planner, urban designer, and principal of Venturi, Scott Brown and Associates, Inc (VSBA). She is a respected theorist, writer and educator, whose work and ideas have influenced architects and planners worldwide. She has being honored with numerous awards and she is co-author with Robert Venturi and Steven Izenour of the influential book *Learning from Las Vegas* (MIT Press, 1972).

Haolun Shu is an independent filmaker and film professor at Shanghai University. He is the director of *Struggle* (2001) and the widely succesful *Nostalgia* (2006), a documentary about Da Zhongli, one of Shanghai's oldest neighborhoods. The film has been in several film festivals and won the Reel China 2006 Best Documentary Award. Haolun Shu obtained his Masters degree in Fine Arts from Southern Illinois University in the United States.

Robert Venturi is an architect and founding principal of Venturi, Scott Brown and Associates, Inc (VSBA). His teaching, lecturing, and writing have received widespread attention and critical review. He has being honored with numerous awards including the Pritzker Architecture Prize in 1991 and the Presidential National Medal of the Arts and 1992. He is co-author with Denise Scott Brown and Steven Izenour of the influential book *Learning from Las Vegas* (MIT Press, 1972).

Xiaochun Zhang received her Ph.D. from Tongji University in 2004. She is the director of the editorial office of Time+Architecture, one of the leading architectural magazines in China. In 2006 she published a book entitled *Cultural Adaptation and Displacement of City Center: A Anthropological Study of Modern Shanghai's Urban Space.*

Acknowledgments

Shanghai Transforming is the result of a collaborative effort, and without each one of the contributions, this book would never have been possible.

I would especially like to thank four people who played a key role in developing this project: Sol Madridejos, Juan Carlos Sancho, Juan de Dios Perez and Andrew Clark.

Sol Madridejos and Juan Carlos Sancho started it all, sharing their exciting experiences in Shanghai and opening my eyes to an incredible city.

Photographer Juan de Dios Perez joined me in my first trip to Shanghai to discover the city together and capture it with a fresh perspective.

Andrew Clark joined me during the development of the book to research and process the information and has since become a key part of it.

Silas Chiow, Philip Enquist, Carlos Ferrater, Greg Girard, Sharon Haar, Jaime Lerner, Xiangning Li & Xiaochun Zhang, Sol Madridejos & Juan Carlos Sancho, Jonathan Miller, Juan de Dios Perez, Weigang Qiu, Peter G. Rowe, Saskia Sassen, Denise Scott Brown, Haolun Shu, and Robert Venturi contributed with their essays and photographs.

Jason Pickleman from JNL Design designed a template that gave order to the incredible amount of information that was produced.

Susan Scanlon, Ariadne dos Santos Daher, Nuria Ayala, Elena Castro, and Emily Lee made possible all the coordination with the contributors.

Casa Asia, through the Ruy de Clavijo 2006 grant, as well as SOM Chicago gave this project the economical and institutional support.

Olvido Gara, Carlos Ferrater, Lluis Hortet, John Nelson, Daniel Friedman and Xavier Vendrell helped me while pursuing funding for the book.

Alejandro Alvar González, Manuela Garcia Pascual, Juan Ignacio Motiloa, Pedro Pablo Arroyo, and Zheng Shiling helped me understand the city the first time I visited it.

Juan Betancur, Edward Cheung, Teresa Foucher, Aaron May, Steven Montgomery, Tim Stelzer, Elena Stevanato, Joshua Wickerham, and BenWoodSTUDIO SHANGHAI contributed with their photographs.

Jenel Farrell, from National Public Radio, and Christl Stoiber from Fritz Stoiber Productions, allowed me to use their information and photographs.

Robert Bruegmann, Alexander Hartray, David Brown, Peter Kindel, Kevin Harrington, and Andrew Dribin gave the right input at the right time.

My special thanks to Gavin Browning and everyone at ACTAR, especially Ramon Prat and Albert Ferré, for making this book a reality.

Finally, my thanks to Julie who has suffered and supported me through this long process. And mostly, to my parents Rafael and Pilar who have always supported and encouraged me to pursue my goals.

To all of you, my most sincere THANK YOU.

Illustration Credits

The author and the publisher have made every effort to obtain proper credit information and permission to reproduce the images. The publisher would be grateful to receive information from any copyright holder not credited herein. Omissions will be corrected in subsequent editions.

Main Photography:

Juan de Dios Perez inside fold-out cover, 2-11, 20-29, 56-63, 67, 80, 86-93, 102-103, 127, 139-149, 153-155, 170-179, 198-203, 212, 214, 220-221, 226-227, 236-239, 246-253

Additional Photography:

Ben Wood Studio Shanghai 210
Bureau of the Shanghai World Expo Coordination 52-53
Edward Cheung 258
Greg Girard 157-159
Iker Gil 46-47, 64-65, 94-95, 116-117, 234-235, 254-255
Jonathan Miller 160
Joshua Wickerham 224-225

Juan Bentancur 54-55, 113
Peter G. Rowe (courtesy of) 76, 78-79
Sancho Madridejos Architecture Office 256
Sharon Haar 72, 75
Skidmore, Owings & Merrill LLP 261-267
Teresa Foucher 68, 71, 183, 222-223
Tim Stelzer 108-109, 218-219
Transrapid International GmbH & Co. KG 44
Yuanmin Lu 150
Xiangning Li & Xiaochun Zhang (courtesy of) 204-207, 209, 211

All images and illustrations not listed above belong to the public domain.

Shanghai Transforming

Published by
Actar

Editor
Iker Gil

Research
Iker Gil
Andrew Clark

Maps & Diagrams
Andrew Clark

Editorial Advice and Copyediting
Gavin Browning

Graphic Design
Jason Pickleman / JNL Graphic Design

Graphic supervision
David Lorente / Actar Pro

Principal Photographer
Juan de Dios Perez

Translation
Ana Ramirez

Production
Actar Pro

Printing
Ingoprint S.A.

ISBN 978-84-96954-66-3
DL B-42.308-2008

Shanghai Transforming has been published
with the help of the Ruy de Clavijo 2006 Grant
awarded anually by **Casa Asia**, Barcelona, Spain.

CASA ASIA

Distribution
ACTAR D
Roca i Batlle 2-4
E-08023 Barcelona
Tel: +34 93 4174993
Fax: +34 93 4186707
office@actar-d.com
www.actar-d.com

Distribution USA
Actar Distribution, Inc.
158 Lafayette St., 5th Floor
New York, NY 10013 USA
Tel: +1 212 966 2207
Fax: +1 212 966 2214
officeusa@actar-d.com
www.actar-d.com